ARCHITECTURE IN AUSTRIA A SURVEY OF THE 20TH CENTURY

Birkhäuser Publishers
Basel · Boston · Berlin

ACTAR Barcelona

This publication was developed in connection with the exhibition "Architecture in Austria. A survey of the 20th Century" in Spain. The exhibition and this book together provide the most comprehensive overview of 20th-century Austrian architecture. The project was made possible by establishing the Architektur Zentrum Wien in 1993. However, one could ask why is an institution needed to mount an exhibition and a publish a book? Simply because these activities are the young institution's main mandate: to discover, collect, and present Austrian architecture and provide information both nationally and internationally. The Architektur Zentrum Wien's activities also focus on serving as the relevant Austrian location, catering to an international network of comparable museums and institutes of architecture, and offering international information exchange for the advancement of architecture.

Both the exhibition and the publication are derived from an extensive architecture database, an archive, and a collection that have been scientifically developed at the Architektur Zentrum Wien and made accessible to the public at large. This base may be restructured and presented to cater to any theme or focus. This took place for the first time in 1995 for a large exhibition at the Deutsches Architektur Museum in Frankfurt. The material has now been reassessed, re-evaluated, and updated.

The Architektur Zentrum Wien wishes to express its thanks particulary to all lenders, institutions, architects and photographers. Special thanks go to the Albertina Graphic Collection, to Shoka/Sevilla, to the Andalusian government, and to the Austrian Ministry of Foreign Affairs who have graciously co-financed the exhibition, and the two publishers ACTAR/Barcelona and Birkhäuser/Basel, without whom this book would not have been possible.

Dietmar Steiner
Director of the Architektur Zentrum Wien

15 **From Viennese Singularity
to Austrian Diversity**
Otto Kapfinger

{ 1 } **A Chronology**
(1900 - 1975)

26 **Architectural Renewal**
(1900 - 1920)

28 **Metropolitan railway**
Otto Wagner
Vienna, 1894

34 **Secession**
Joseph Maria Olbrich
Vienna, 1897–98

38 **Apartment and commercial building
Portois & Fix**
Max Fabiani
Vienna, 1899–1900

42 **Church of St Leopold**
Otto Wagner
Vienna, 1902–07

46 **Zacherl House**
Josef Plecnik
Vienna, 1903–05

50 **Postal Savings Bank**
Otto Wagner
Vienna, 1904

54 **Sanatorium Westend**
Josef Hoffmann
Purkersdorf, Lower Austria, 1904

56 **Michaeler House**
Adolf Loos
Vienna, 1910

60 **Modernism and "Heimat"**
(1920 - 1945)

62 **Crematorium**
Clemens Holzmeister
Vienna, 1921–23

64 **Wittgenstein House**
Paul Engelmann, Ludwig Wittgenstein
Vienna, 1926–28

66 **Karl-Marx-Hof**
Karl Ehn
Vienna, 1926–30

70 **Ebensee Secondary School**
Julius Schulte
Ebensee, Upper Austria, 1927

72 **Moller House**
Adolf Loos
Vienna, 1927–28

76 **Northern Cable Railway**
Franz Baumann
Innsbruck, Tyrol, 1927–28

80 **Substation Favoriten**
Eugen Kastner, Fritz Waage
Vienna, 1928–31

82 **Beer House**
Josef Frank, Oskar Wlach
Vienna, 1929–31

86 **Tobacco Factory**
Peter Behrens, Alexander Popp
Linz, Upper Austria, 1929–35

90 **Liesing Labour Office**
Ernst Anton Plischke
Vienna, 1930–32

92 **Werkbundsiedlung**
Josef Frank (project leader)
Vienna, 1930–32

96 **Heyrovsky House**
Lois Welzenbacher
Zell am See, Salzburg, 1932

98 **Gamerith House**
Ernst Anton Plischke
Seewalchen, Upper Austria, 1933-34

102 **Girls' Secondary School**
Hans Steineder
Attnang Puchheim, Upper Austria, 1934-35

104 **Grossglockner Alpine Road**
Franz Wallack
Salzburg/Carinthia, 1930-35

106 **Displacement and Progress**
(1945 - 1975)

108 **Schweizerspende Kindergarten**
Franz Schuster
Vienna, 1948-49

110 **Gänsehäufel Beach Facility**
Max Fellerer, Eugen Wörle
Vienna, 1948-50

112 **Fair pavilion Felten & Guilleaume**
Oswald Haerdtl
Vienna, 1951-53

114 **Sports Hall**
Roland Rainer
Vienna, 1952-58, 1971-74, 1994

118 **Pastoral Counselling Centre Ennsleiten**
Arbeitsgruppe 4 [Wilhelm Holzbauer, Friedrich Kurrent, Johannes Spalt] and Johann Georg Gsteu
Steyr, Upper Austria, 1958-61

120 **Church of St Therese**
Rudolf Schwarz
Linz, Upper Austria, 1958-62

122 **Museum of the 20th Century**
Karl Schwanzer
Vienna, 1959-62

124 **Counselling Centre Baumgarten**
Johann Georg Gsteu
Vienna, 1960-65

126 **Candle Shop Retti**
Hans Hollein
Vienna, 1964-65

128 **Dreifaltigkeit Church**
Fritz Wotruba, Fritz G. Mayr
Vienna, 1965-76

130 **Garden City**
Roland Rainer
Puchenau near Linz, Upper Austria, 1963-95

132 **Felsenbad**
Gerhard Garstenauer
Badgastein, Salzburg, 1967-68

134 **Provincial ORF studio**
Gustav Peichl
Salzburg, 1968-72

138 **Juridicum**
Ernst Hiesmayr
Vienna, 1968-84

140 **A City for Children**
Anton Schweighofer
Vienna, 1969-74

142 **Ruhwiesen Housing Project**
Rudolf Wäger
Schlins, Vorarlberg, 1971-73

144 **Zentralsparkasse Bank Floridsdorf Branch Office**
Johannes Spalt, Friedrich Kurrent
Vienna, 1970-74

[2] Spectrum of the Present
(from 1975 onwards)

146 The panorama

148 **Zentralsparkasse Bank Favoriten Branch**
Günther Domenig
Vienna, 1975–79

150 **Salvador Church**
Johannes Spalt
Vienna, 1976–79

152 **Greenhouses Institute of Botany**
Volker Giencke
Graz, Styria, 1982–93

154 **Stone House**
Günther Domenig
Steindorf, Carinthia, as of 1986

158 **Bene Administration and Factory**
Ortner & Ortner
Waidhofen, Lower Austria, 1986–88

160 **Office Building**
Coop Himmelb(l)au
Seibersdorf, Lower Austria, 1993–95

164 **Graz Airport**
Florian Riegler, Roger Riewe
Graz, Styria, 1992–94

170 **Absberggasse Basic Secondary School**
Rüdiger Lainer
Vienna, 1992–94

172 **Kink-Platz Basic Secondary School**
Helmut Richter
Vienna, 1992–95

176 **M. House**
Hermann Czech
Schwechat, Lower Austria, 1977–81

178 **Duplex House Glanegg**
Max Rieder
Groedig, Salzburg, 1990–92

180 **Provincial Vocational College**
Dietmar Eberle, Karl Baumschlager
Bregenz, Vorarlberg, 1993–94

182 **Power Station**
Marie-Claude Bétrix, Eraldo Consolascio,
Eric Maier with Guido Züger
Salzburg, 1992–95

184 **Design Centre**
Thomas Herzog
Linz, Upper Austria, 1988, 1991–93

186 **Auditorium**
Klaus Kada
St. Pölten, Lower Austria, 1992–97

190 **Federal Library & Archives of Lower Austria**
Karin Bily, Paul Katzberger, Michael Loudon
St. Pölten, Lower Austria, 1992–97

194 **Zehdengasse Elementary School**
ARTEC [Bettina Götz, Richard Manahl]
Vienna, 1995–96

196 The Beautiful Landscape

198 **Faculty of Natural Sciences**
Wilhelm Holzbauer
Salzburg, 1982–86

200 **Mountain Chapel**
Friedrich Kurrent
Ramingstein, Salzburg, 1990–91

202 **Kolig House**
Manfred Kovatsch
Ossiacher Lake, Carinthia, 1975–77

204 **Sports Gymnasium**
Othmar Barth
Stams, Tyrol, 1977-82

206 **Bartenbach Light Studio**
Josef Lackner
Aldrans, Tyrol, 1986-88

208 **Lakeside Facility Häupl**
Maximilian Luger, Franz Maul
Attersee Lake, Upper Austria, 1990-91

210 **Primary and Basic Secondary School**
Roland Gnaiger
Warth, Vorarlberg, 1991-92

212 **Hotel Vier Jahreszeiten and Alpinhotel**
Alois and Elena Neururer
Mandarfen, Tyrol, 1991-92

214 **Silvretta House**
Much Untertrifaller jr, Gerhard Hörburger
Bielerhöhe, Vorarlberg, 1991-92

216 **Footbridge over the Mur**
Marcel Meili, Markus Peter, Jürg Conzett
Murau, Styria, 1993-95

220 **GucklHupf**
Hans-Peter Wörndl
Lake Mondsee, Salzburg, 1993

224 **Studio for a Musician and Composer**
Margarethe Heubacher-Sentobe
Weerberg-Innerst, Tyrol, 1995-96

228 **Golmerbahn**
Leopold Kaufmann
Vandans, Vorarlberg, 1995

230 **An Historical Location**

232 **Dirmhirngasse Basic Secondary School**
Boris Podrecca
Vienna, 1992-94

234 **Roof Construction Project Falkestrasse**
Coop Himmelb(l)au
Vienna, 1983-88

236 **Extension Project Laboratory Hall**
Bernhard Hafner
Leoben, Styria, 1990-92

238 **Haas House**
Hans Hollein
Vienna, 1985-90

240 **Computer Centre**
Riepl + Moser
Hagenberg, Upper Austria, 1986-89

242 **Glass Museum**
Klaus Kada
Baernbach, Styria, 1987-88

244 **Arts Centre**
Konrad Frey
Mürzzuschlag, Styria, 1988-91

246 **Museumsquartier**
Ortner & Ortner
Vienna, since 1990

248 **Kunsthalle Art Centre**
Adolf Krischanitz
Krems, Lower Austria, 1993-95

250 **Town Theatre & Cinema**
Heinz Tesar
Hallein, Salzburg, since 1991

252 **Celtic Museum**
Heinz Tesar
Hallein, Salzburg, since 1991

254 **Regional Exhibition**
Günther Domenig
Hüttenberg, Carinthia, 1993-95

256 **Kleines Café**
Hermann Czech
Vienna, 1970, 1973-74, 1985

258 **City Hall** (reconstruction)
Ernst Beneder
Waidhofen/Ybbs, Lower Austria, 1994-95

260 **Generali Foundation**
Christian Jabornegg, András Pálffy
Vienna, 1993-95

262 **Penthouse**
Rüdiger Lainer
Vienna, 1994-95

264 **Jewish Museum**
Eichinger oder Knechtl
Vienna, 1995-96

266 **Arts Centre**
Peter Zumthor
Bregenz, Vorarlberg, 1994-97

272 **Public Housing**

274 **Housing Project Pumpligahn**
Norbert Fritz
Innsbruck, Tyrol, 1986-88,1994-95

275 **Housing Project Wuhrbaumweg**
Mike Loudon, Markus Koch
Bregenz, Vorarlberg, 1988-90

276 **Housing Project Im Fang**
Dietmar Eberle, Markus Koch,
Wolfgang Juen, Norbert Mittersteiner
Höchst, Vorarlberg, 1978-79

277 **Housing Project Wienerberger Gründe**
Ralph Erskine, Hubert Riess
Graz, Styria, 1982-87

278 **Housing Project Brunner Strasse**
Helmut Richter
Vienna, 1986-91

282 **Housing Project Knittelfeld**
Michael Szyszkowitz, Karla Kowalski
Knittelfeld, Styria 1988-92

284 **Housing Project Pilotengasse**
Adolf Krischanitz,
Jacques Herzog & Pierre de Meuron,
Otto Steidle + Partner
Vienna, 1989-92

286 **Housing Project Seiersberg**
Manfred Wolff-Plottegg
Graz, Styria, 1987-91

288 **Apartment Building
Frauenfelderstrasse**
Dieter Henke, Martha Schreieck
Vienna, 1990-93

292 **Housing Project Strassgang**
Florian Riegler, Roger Riewe
Graz, Styria, 1992-94

294 **Lodging House Matznergasse
"Coffin factory"**
BKK-2
Vienna, 1994-96

298 **"Viennese Loft"**
Heidulf Gerngross - Werkstatt Wien
Vienna, 1996-97

302 **Housing Project Hödlwald**
Splitterwerk
Bürmoos, Salzburg, 1994-96

306 **Housing Project Ölzbündt**
Hermann Kaufmann
Dornbirn, Vorarlberg, 1997

309 **Biographies**

333 **Photo credits**

From Viennese Singularity to Austrian Diversity

OTTO KAPFINGER

Is there some kind of thread running through the last hundred years of Austria's architecture? Are there specific perspectives that can be found only here, nowhere else? What characteristic contributions has this country made to architecture around the world? The search for some possible underlying pattern in Austria's last hundred years will obviously encounter some difficulties. The thread may be there – at least it has a clear and strong beginning – but its continuity has been forcefully interrupted several times, and it becomes frayed, is almost lost, then resumed, intertwines with other threads and is now a fractional, multicoloured kaleidoscope.

The factual situation: the school founded and inspired by Otto Wagner was a central forum for architectural renewal, enjoying both European significance and global fame between 1895 and 1912: apart from Wagner, there were also Joseph Maria Olbrich, Josef Hoffmann, Adolf Loos, Max Fabiani, Joze Plecnik, Jan Kotera and Friedrich Ohmann working in Vienna. At the turn of the century it was the capital of a multinational monarchy with 60 million inhabitants. Richard Neutra joined Wagner's school; Rudolf Schindler studied under Loos and Wagner; Oskar Strnad, Josef Frank, and Hubert Gessner carried out their first building projects in 1913.

The complexity and contradictory nature of Wagner's oeuvre – full of imagery and metaphors but also very structural and typological – or of Olbrich's Secession, which combines the Apollinian and Dionysian, new structural plasticity and new ornaments, archaic-mythical forms and modern multifunctionalism of the floor plan under the industrial glass roofs, or Adolf Loos's house at Michaelerplatz, show why this architectural renewal in Vienna cannot be explained in simple terms. The latter project is virtually a concentrate of well-calculated complexity, a combination of absolutely innovative spatial solutions with completely disparate facades: classical representation and bourgeois simplicity facing the square on the one hand and best "Chicago industrial construction" facing the courtyard on the other.

In this climate of lush cultural growth, so characteristic of the Danube metropolis, the chains of historicism were broken and ideas that were to become reality in the classical "Moderne" some 10 to 15 years later were being written down in the Wagner school lab. Moreover,

Loos, Frank, and Strnad had already formulated their progressive criticism of this "Moderne" before 1914. They refuse any adherence to a new, universal style and express their scepticism of any culture aiming to establish formal uniformity.

Loos turns out to be the fiercest critic of the founding of the Deutsche Werkbund (German Craft Federation) in 1907. This does not, however, prevent the foundation of the Austrian Werkbund (Austrian Craft Federation) by Josef Hoffmann soon after.

1918 brings a deep caesura. The monarchy disintegrates into national states. With its "inflated" capital Vienna, Austria loses its most significant industrial and agricultural hinterland including Bohemia, Moravia and Hungary; the imperial city becomes social-democratic Red Vienna. Under extremely difficult economic conditions, housing projects for the working class become the central theme in all building activities. While the avant-garde in Germany or France are concerned with the industrialization of construction and mass housing projects, no-one in Austria takes on this issue for lack of a technologically experienced large-scale industry. In Vienna, however, the large brickyards dating back to the age of royal and imperial patronage continue to exist while masses of unemployed workers eke out an existence. This leads to the emergence of large housing projects financed by the City of Vienna in line with very conventional construction technology – quite in contrast to the reformatory programme of a New Frankfurt. However, the "Wiener Siedlerbewegung" architectural movement emerged even before the Karl-Marx-Hof was built and the technological experiments of Bauhaus had been carried out. Loos, Frank and others planned numerous housing projects here before 1923 that were actually carried out by using the most primitive means and with the extensive participation of the future inhabitants in the framework of cooperatives highly advanced as regards grass-roots, political, cultural, and educational aspects. Loos's famous patent "house with wall" is an ideal strategy that ingeniously uses simple, existing resources as a system and combines these with a liberal attitude to individual inhabitant participation in the construction process, the growth potential of the house, an intensive relationship to the utility garden and the harnessing of solar energy. The actual experience in the pioneering age of the "Wiener Siedlerbewegung" also explains Loos's and Frank's critical distance to the rather academic experiments of Le Corbusier or Bauhaus and to their tendency of creating consistent, new worlds to live in "from top-down". Technologically, the "Wiener Werkbundsiedlung" adheres to conventions; as regards its spatial typology however, it offers a rich, pluralistic panorama of possibilities. In his villas, Frank opens Loos's closed-off concept to house and garden, linking the interior with the exterior in a figure of movement; Ernst Plischke and Lois Welzenbacher use the reflections of the landscape, the specific topography to create their own individual, new, plastic house organization.

In the years 1933/34 the next caesura occurs – in parallel to Germany: cultural liberalism and social democracy meet a violent end; in the corporate state, Clemens Holzmeister is sporadically able to continue his popular, expressive iconographic style. In 1938, when National Socialists assume power in Austria, – he also remains in Turkish exile.

At this point in time, more than one third of the 70 architects participating in the "Wiener Werkbundsiedlung" had been forced to leave the country; hardly any of them were to return after 1945.

To trace and continue the development of Austrian architecture after 1945 is a difficult task. In the provincial climate of this period – bereft of its intellectual elite due to emigration and the Holocaust – the emerging generation had to find its roots again and re-establish its contacts to the international scene.

In the liberal climate of the Holzmeister school, several young architects with different personalities emerge (Friedrich Achleitner, Johann Gsteu, Hans Hollein, Wilhelm Holzbauer, Friedrich Kurrent, Josef Lackner, Gustav Peichl, Anton Schweighofer, Johannes Spalt etc.) whose positions even today – as established and almost historical – constitute the background for contemporary architecture. Roland Rainer (on his own) recreates the link between the Wiener Gartenstadtbewegung (garden city movement) and the related fields of international housing and urban planning debates. In Austria, he becomes successful only after many years. For the team Arbeitsgruppe 4 and their entourage, the meeting with Konrad Wachsmann at the summer academies in Salzburg turn out to be particularly productive. Inspired and shaped by his constructive and structural systematics, buildings and projects emerge that overcome the schematicism of the late international style by visually activated construction and the highly developed, tense polyvalence of spatial structures.

In reaction to this rather anti-symbolic, anti-formal, structural approach so characteristic of Loos, Hans Hollein continues to develop Holzmeister's strong representative and highly symbolic approach – inspired by his international experience in the world of art. In the early 1960s, two great cultural traditions in Austria leave their mark on architecture: the baroque, mannerist, complex representative art and effect of the formal approach – and the enlightened tradition critical of language and form under the influence of Karl Kraus, Ernst Mach and Ludwig Wittgenstein.

In 1958 Achleitner, Gsteu, Kurrent and Spalt join Wachsmann in Salzburg; Hollein meets Friedrich Kiesler in New York and encounters the work of Rudolf Schindler in California. In 1958, Josef Frank writes his last sublime text, "Accidentism", in which he summarizes his aversion towards any programme of style. In 1958 Günther Feuerstein writes his "Theses on incidental architecture". In 1958 Roland Rainer is appointed Urban Planner of Vienna, but resigns four years later. This prepared the Viennese scenario of the 1960s. This climate bred the liberal and radical scene of Graz' architecture – stimulated especially by the partnership between Günther Domenig and Eilfried Huth – and under the leadership of Hollein, Pichler, and Feuerstein the experimental groups – Haus-Rucker-Co, Coop Himmelblau, Missing Link, etc. – were founded – in critical dialogue with the new generation of Plischke, Rainer and Peichl students.

The end of bohemianism. Scenes of Austrian architecture since 1975

The mid-1970s mark the trough of a wave. The technological and social visions of the late '70s were deprived of its economic base by the oil crisis. While the utopian ideas of the groups Haus-Rucker-Co, Coop Himmelb(l)au, Missing Link, Zündup etc. were nowhere near being realized, post-modernism, which was lagging behind, was being overtaken both left and right. The aging post-war avant-garde, against whose conformist ethics and morals the angry movement of '68 had rebelled, were given the opportunity of showing and internationally promoting their work retrospectively in the extensive exhibition "Austrian Architecture 1945-75" in Vienna. However, this retrospective came at a time when the most significant innovations of the '50s and '60s – especially in church and school construction – had already subsided and when the yet small number of domestic architects still held outsider positions in relation to the country's political, bureaucratic and economic forces. It may be symptomatic for the small group of committed architects, which had considerably contributed to architecture between 1945 and 1975 – the Austrian Society for Architecture – to suffer heavy crisis immediately afterwards and come close to being dissolved. While the "old avant-garde" looked back onto a small but compact high-quality oeuvre of buildings, contemporary architecture was still considered incomprehensibly exotic within the relevant playing field of public and cooperative building developers. In 1970, the competition for the construction of the UN dependency in Vienna, the largest international architecture competition ever to be organized in the country, opted for an extremely mediocre "Austrian solution" after shady wrangling for national prestige and contract sinecures. In spite of being appointed to academic positions and commissioned to build numerous objects, the "old avant-garde" - Friedrich Kurrent, Johannes Spalt, Gustav Peichl, Hans Hollein, Ottokar Uhl, Anton Schweighofer, Josef Lackner, Johann Georg Gsteu etc. – constituted a fringe group around 1975, while the "new avant-garde" of the time was forced to withdraw from the active areas of the media and university to the lighter and more effectively playable field of art.

Twenty years later, much has changed. It seems at least that the emphasis has shifted. The advanced field of construction has experienced explosive growth; it has a brilliant portfolio of project realizations to show; some of the architects enjoy star status in the media; and in contrast to worse days when ministerial arbitrariness and the dominating schematicism of building developers in the '70s prevailed, large-scale public contracts are now also tied in to high-quality selection processes. The avant-garde of the '60s was able to add an extensive batch of oeuvres in the past decade. And two new generations emerged from its long shadow, the older of which has found its way from the bohemianism of the '70s to professional work in the '80s and finally emancipated themselves from the moralizing pressure of their predecessors and teachers, while the younger generation did not hesitate to demand its own share of building projects with international self-assurance.

This may all be merely a regionally tainted and rough version of the paradigm shift in the European scene as a whole. As regards transregional developments however, several main events that were specific and decisive for the Austrian situation must be mentioned here. In Styria, initial impulses for structural change were set in 1975. The law on housing construction was revised in such a manner that since then, public subsidies have been tied to architectural competitions as soon as projects involve 50 apartments or more. In parallel, the Styrian provincial construction authorities have not carried out "Amtsplanungen", that is official planning, for building construction since 1978. Instead, it was decided to carry out the entire range of public building projects – from hospitals and universities to the smallest renovation projects of existing official buildings – through carefully tendered competitions and direct assignments to selected architects. Moreover, in 1980, the "Modell Steiermark" was adopted, earmarking a share of the budget for subsidized housing expressly for the exemplary use of innovative and experimental planning. Undoubtedly, the personal commitment of the Styrian provincial governor, Mr. Josef Krainer, for contemporary architecture and the work of Wolfdieter Dreibholz in the construction department of the provincial government played a decisive role in promoting these reforms. The phenomenal development of the "Grazer Schule" far beyond the conventional sector of private contractors and sporadically interested economic players would have been impossible without these unique structural conditions and political support "from above". To complete the picture, Günther Domenig, the most pronounced leading figure of young architecture in Graz was asked to teach at the University of Technology in Graz in 1980. A declared anti-institutionalist school established the official teaching of a non-conformist approach that had grown in the liberty of its legendary "drawing studios".

It took a long time before comparable developments began in Vienna. Vienna was able to counter the Styrian realization rate only with theoretical discourse. In 1979, after a generation replacement had occurred in the Austrian Society for Architecture and the foundation of the magazine "UMBAU" an intensive discussion began between the simultaneous movements in Switzerland, Germany, Italy and the USA. The permanent proactive coverage of architecture in Vienna's print media resulted directly from these efforts. Around 1980, it was easy to believe that the city of Vienna had long been complete. The old buildings of the Danube monarchy were like an oversized coat in which contemporary efforts were overtaxed simply when attempting to preserve existing building stock, where promising projects could only become manifest in ephemeral, miniature or homeopathic rereadings of the status quo. A change in social housing resulted from the Erwin Wippel initiative, a clever estate agent, who from 1981 radically trimmed the schematic routine of sclerotic housing cooperatives. The "GWV – Gesellschaft für Wohnungs –, Wirtschafts- und Verkehrswesen", a special coordination office, was established to gather unconventional architects, some well-known, some extremely young, and bring them together with the hitherto profit-oriented building developers. Their pilot project Biberhaufenweg began in 1981.

In spite of its small dimensions, this just-in-time project seemed very programmatic in the long smouldering housing debate and was also such a media success that the hypothesis that the social-democratic Municipality reacted to improve quality in their housing production proves true. The "GWV" initiated almost all projects that rank among the highlights of Vienna's housing construction activities in the 1980s. In the Danube city, housing construction has also been the only niche, for almost a decade, where internationally acknowledged architecture was built other than the cherished small-scale art of shop, restaurant, and villa construction, which simply had to be conserved. The quality debate in the large field of urban, commercial, and representative projects in Vienna was not reestablished until Vienna reacted to the already well-established development of "city competition" in Western Europe and "new urbanism", the appointment of Hannes Swoboda as Vienna's councillor for city planning in 1988, and the new growth perspectives emerging with the fall of the Iron Curtain.

In Styria, after the initial impulse had been ensured by the "reforms from top-down", starting from the centre of political power, the possibly even more comprehensive and more radical "Salzburg-Projekt" emerged as a surprising coup organized by a peripheral protest movement against established conditions. With the success of his party "Bürgerliste", Johannes Voggenhuber became planning councillor in Salzburg in 1982. Thanks to his competence as a member of the construction authority, his architectural expertise, and know-how in spatial planning, he was able to begin with radical architectural reforms. Salzburg, a community with a unique historical cityscape, but also with much red tape in its construction policy and glaring eyesores of modern urban planning, was to become a model for the restructuring of a "European city". With the support of an advisory council, the "Gestaltungsbeirat", which was founded in 1983, Voggenhuber was able to carry out some notable projects and involve numerous well-known domestic and foreign architects – the first situation of its kind in decades. Overnight, architecture and urbanism had become subject to intensive, partly tough and populist, partly highly-qualified public discussion in Salzburg. The idea of the advisory council was modified, updated, and adopted by several other provincial capitals, including Vienna, Vorarlberg, Upper and Lower Austria. Voggenhuber's commitment, which confronted him with the deplorable economic, political, and cultural situation, was no longer rewarded in the following elections. However, his impulses have helped resuscitate the local discussion on architecture to this day. His tenure has left behind some significant buildings and ideas with transregional influence.

In western Austria the situation is somewhat different again. The sell-out of landscape and Alpine building traditions to promote tourism has passed the point of no return in Tyrol. Relative wealth has, however, always guaranteed the talented individuals among architects a constant inflow of contracts from private building developers. Around 1990, the architectural scene also began to open - focused by the discussion platform of the "Architekturforum Tirol" - an emancipation from the "autochthonous" dialogue with the classics of the regional "Moderne" and self-assured participation of young architects in international discourse. Unconventional building clients from commerce, industry, and tourism at least partially opened up fields that had been lying completely fallow.

Vorarlberg is a special case – not only in Austria. The "Vorarlberger Bauschule", which was known far beyond the horizon of the technical world, was no school in the conventional fashion. In contrast to Styria or to the "Salzburg-Projekt", it involved the gradual development of a solidarity movement for rational, modern, economical building "from bottom-up". Outside the universities and far away from the cultural and bureaucratic establishment, this was an activity that from the beginning was determined not solely by architects but chiefly by building developers. Having grown up in the alternative movement, these "building artists" of the 1980s have succeeded in establishing a broad effect. They have penetrated even the middle class, and conventional social and cooperative housing. This way, a "subcutaneous" climate of architecture evolved in the "Ländle", the provincial countryside, without official support, where in the late '80s small housing and single-family house construction was able to break out of its niche and win many competitions, playing a significant role in the entire area of public and large-scale building contracts. If there is a date that is significant for this development, it would be somewhere during the late '70s: in 1978 the cooperative in Dornbirn began its activities. Its dynamics greatly promoted cheap community housing, and the architects who emerged from the cooperative also contributed greatly to the opening of the field for larger contracts and the internationalization of the Vorarlberg phenomenon.

In all that has been said thus far, neither the oeuvres of individual architects nor the actual architectural positions in the country have been addressed. In view of Austria's discernable diversity of interesting contemporary buildings, the historical "exterior" scaffolding of the growth conditions that gave rise to this manifoldness must be explained before entering into an analysis of domestic architecture, which can merely be touched on briefly. For both the Viennese and the Grazer scene the major shifts take place around 1986/87. In Vienna, the generation of those now in their 50s freed itself from the all too absorbing omnipresent traditions and unfolds a panorama of highly differentiated positions. Helmut Richter is assigned the housing project Brunnerstrasse by the "GWV"; Coop Himmelb(l)au wins the expertise procedure for the Ronacher Theatre and works on the roof construction project Falkestrasse; Adolf Krischanitz builds the housing project Pilotengasse together with Herzog & de Meuron and Otto Steidle; Heinz Tesar designs the central office of Schömer GmbH; Rüdiger Lainer and Gertraud Auer are commissioned for their first large-scale projects and the public media competition for the Haas House by Hans Hollein on St Stephen's Square is decided in his favour only after the construction panels had been placed and the foundation pit excavated.

At the same time, Graz turns away from exuberant baroque expression, from the heroic struggle against conventions to elegant objectivity. In 1988, the young ARTEC team wins the competition for the construction authority building in Graz with a laconic and completely unromantic contribution. The individual signatures of Günther Domenig, Klaus Kada, Volker Giencke, Konrad Frey, or Szyszkowitz/Kowalski can no longer be absorbed within the label "Grazer Schule". In Vorarlberg, Carlo Baumschlager/Dietmar Eberle break with their timber phase and begin to work with the new German-Swiss architecture at immense speed and proceed to win several large-scale competitions; Roland Gnaiger and Hermann Kaufmann carry out their first large-scale projects.

If one were to continue and attempt to classify today's outstanding architects and their oeuvre in Austria – this would involve more than 100 names – one would be doomed to failure. The generation of architects over 60 today include such well-matured personal styles as that of Hans Hollein, whose complex narration unmistakably amalgamates the entire international development since 1960 against the backdrop of Vienna's special psychological and display art; or Günther Domenig, who formally and conceptually broadens and quantitatively enriches his transformation of the organic, so characteristic of his expression in the '70s; or Gustav Peichl, whose symbolic technicisms have evolved to become clear versions of the classical "Moderne"; or Josef Lackner, whose original, plastic building objects have always featured specific lighting, and who continues with this theme even in his most recent application of new technologies in "late" masterpieces; or Wilhelm Holzbauer, whose talent in creating large spatial and formal organizations results in a well-calculated routine of the last decade, in view of the flood of contracts.

For the generation of architects aged around 50, a rough survey successfully differentiates between "neo-modern" and "trans-modern" positions, the former investigating and promoting the technical and conceptual positivism of the classical "Moderne" and the latter finding individual ways to break with the purist idealism of the "Moderne". In Vienna, Coop Himmelb(l)au and their intuitive dynamism stand for the "trans-modern" position – Wolf D. Prix and Helmut Swiczinsky rank among the flag holders and global stars of deconstructivism – then Laurids and Manfred Ortner and their cool realism of urban signs, Adolf Krischanitz and his subversions of the minimal, Rüdiger Lainer and his poetry of incongruencies, or the young team The Office with its median energy of surfaces. In Graz there are Manfred Wolff-Plottegg's ambiguous studies of digital design or the complex simplicity of the duo Florian Riegler-Roger Riewe, Salzburg sports the high culture/low-tech projects by Manfred Max

Rieder. Hermann Czech's thorough analysis of the banal, Boris Podrecca's orchestral continuity of architectural narration, or Heinz Tesar's archaics of body shapes seem to escape such classification but are surely characterized by their critical distance to the solutions of the classical "Moderne". In Vienna, the "neo-modern" position includes Helmut Richter's radical constructivism, Rudolf Prohazka's constructed site diagrams, Elsa Prochazka's precision of subtle interventions, Michael Loudon's structural concepts of space, the sensitive simplicity of works by Eichinger or Knechtl, as well as the technical aesthetics of Driendl+Steixner, the open, clear spatial sequences of Dieter Henke/Martha Scheieck or the abstractions of gravity in the Pauzenberger-Hofstätter designs. In Graz, comparable positions are represented by Klaus Kada's sublime layers of spatial transparency, Volker Giencke's playful humanization of high-tech, or Konrad Frey's often underestimated, fine economy of technology. The list of names is by no means exhaustive. In Vienna the list could continue with Paul Katzberger/Karin Bily, Andreas Fellerer/Jiri Vrendl with Christian Jabornegg/András Pállfy, Walter Stelzhammer; or the architecture collective in Graz including Ernst Giselbrecht, Hubert Riess, Bernhard Hafner, Irmfried Windbichler or Manfred Zernig; in Vorarlberg with Dietrich/Untertrifaller, Bruno Spagolla or Wolfgang Ritsch; in Tyrol with Jörg Streli, Peter Lorenz, Norbert Fritz or Wolfgang Pöschl; in Carinthia with Felix Orsini Rosenberg or Sonja Gasparin; in Salzburg with the Halle 1 team and Fritz Lorenz; in Upper Austria with the duo Riepl/Moser; in Lower Austria with Ernst Beneder – and many more contributions, especially by the younger generation, would still remain unmentioned.

The opening sentence referring to the end of bohemianism is confirmed by the obvious increase in the number of protagonists whose turn to build comes quickly. The struggle to survive is especially strong among the younger and up-and-coming talents, since the number of open competitions has dramatically decreased since 1995.

Recently, commitment in Styria has diminished dramatically - the experimental housing programme has been put on hold. In the "architecture provinces" Carinthia, Lower Austria, and Burgenland however, the foundation of local centres and discussion fora brought new impetus. Five years ago, an initiative such as the school building programme "Schulbauprogramm 2000" carried out between 1991 and 1996 in Vienna would have been unthinkable – now with the departure of City Councillor Swoboda it has become history. The problem today is not that willing building developers dispose of uncongenial planners or that large-scale public construction contracts cannot find the ideal project through appropriate competitions. The problem – in view of the cultural struggle instigated by political populism and the austerity program adopted everywhere in the mid '90s – is the risk involved in promoting contemporary architecture in public. Examples are the drastically curtailed "Museumsquartier" by Ortner & Ortner and the world exhibition project in Vienna, that failed to qualify in a plebiscite, the long delayed Trigon Museum in Graz, the farce of the Guggenheim Museum in Salzburg and Vienna, and the victory celebrated by historicizing conservationism in rebuilding the gutted Redoutensäle of the Vienna Hofburg – just to name a few of the most obvious cases.

Austria's architecture in the late 20th century is surely less marked by technological innovation than in other countries. This can be explained by the lack of historically developed broader base of a matured building industry on the one hand and by the prevailing restrictive, anti-innovative building laws and bureaucratic tradition on the other. The positive side of the claim to conceptual, intellectual architecture reaching beyond everydayness is the undogmatic diversity of precise architectural solutions for highly varied contexts and the creative humour that successfully bridges structural deficits, achieving performances of transregional significance. In Austria, the potential for first-class architecture at the end of this century is probably as grand and diverse as in a larger context during the heroic "golden" age of the turn of the last century. I would even say that the distribution of forces in the federal provinces is much more evenly balanced and explosive than in the days of Otto Wagner. Even if the creation of individual theories is less clear and selective than in other places, the situation does reflect the global tendencies from post-minimalism to post-functionalism and ecological approaches in a highly specific and original manner - supported by a tight network of public presentation and discussion fora and vigorous journalism specialized in architecture, not only in technical publications but also in the mass media.

Today, the historical "Wiener Moderne" is contrasted by the contemporary panorama of "Architecture in Austria", which is as rich, diverse and contrasting as the densely set variations and changes, contradictions and transitions of Austria's landscape itself.

This is the first book for the reader abroad that pays tribute to Austria's contribution to the architecture of the twentieth century. One hundred selected buildings help to illustrate the roots, traditions and changing circumstances of modern architecture in this country. Not only historical, but also contemporary, forward-looking developments in Austrian architectural history are documented in this book. An overall impression of the building process is provided by more than 700 documents, including photographs, sketches and plans. The question of Austria's particular contribution is the topic of discussion in this chronologically and thematically structured review. The aim is not to describe a form of uniqueness, but to reveal regional layers, focal points and responsibilities within in this "trans-national" field.

The book is divided into two sections: <u>A Chronology</u> from 1900 to 1975 and <u>Spectrum of the Present</u>, in which there is a presentation of particularly prominent regional and conceptual issues in Austrian contemporary architecture from 1975 to the present day.

A Chronology
1900 - 1975

Architectural Renewal (1900 - 1920)

Modernism and "Heimat" (1920 - 1945)

Displacement and Progress (1945 - 1975)

{ 1 }

Architectural Renewal (1900 - 1920)

Vienna, 1900. The encroaching demise of the Austro-Hungarian Empire leads to the first manifestations of modernist art: the Vienna City Railway forms the transport-engineering backbone of Otto Wagner's vision of an endless big city, while his church in Steinhof reflects the complex splendour of the Habsburg Empire for the last time. Then, his postoffice savings bank already displays an uncompromising realization of modern-age space. Max Fabiani and Josef Plecnik undertake an exemplary treatment of the question of the separation of skin from bone, and Loos revives the relationships between space, construction and appearance. On the one hand, there is Joseph Maria Olbrich's construction of an archaic temple for the secessionist art avant-garde, but on the other hand, Josef Hoffmann's sanatorium in Purkersdorf heralds the arrival of cubist rationale. In Vienna in 1900, modernist art is celebrated equally as an affliction and as liberation, not as a destructive process, but as an architectural renewal.

Anything created in the modern age must be suitable for new materials and meet contemporary needs, if it is to be appropriate for the modern-day person. It must illustrate our own improved, democratic, self-confident, our keen-minded substance. It must encompass our colossal technical and scientific achievements as well as humankind's unswerving practical nature – of this, there can be no doubt. OTTO WAGNER

We don't sit like this because a carpenter has constructed a chair in such and such a fashion, rather, the carpenter makes the chair like this because we want to sit in such and such a way. ADOLF LOOS

The "technical" projects for the infrastructure of the Austro-Hungarian Empire's capital, with a population of two million, triggered the actual shift in Otto Wagner's work to modernism. The metropolitan railway line cut through the uneven landscape of Vienna's suburbs, partly above ground, partly underground. The Stadtbahn's (metropolitan railway) "gates" at the underground stations and "bridges" at the stations above ground define mass traffic as an aesthetic experience of the modern urban landscape.

Metropolitan railway
Otto Wagner
Vienna, 1894

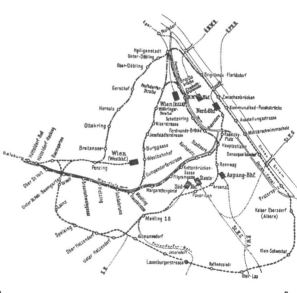

1. Bridge over Wienzeile [photo: M.S.]
2. Urban train map, around 1910

3

4

5

3. Typical underground station of the Wiental line:
cross section, longitudinal section, plan [C.A.A.]
4. Typical underground station, main facade [C.A.A.]
5. Karlsplatz station, historical photograph [photo: H.M.,V.]
6. Schönbrunn underground station [photo: M.S.]

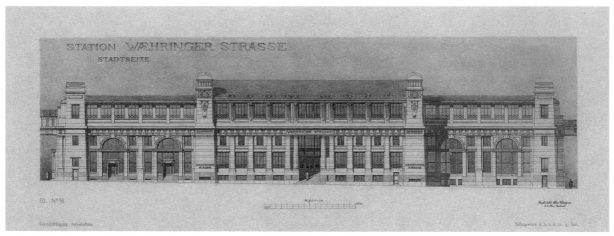

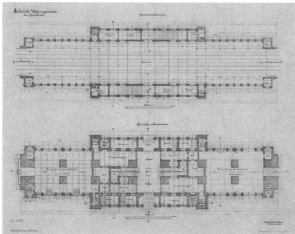

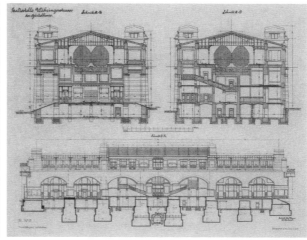

7. Währingerstrasse station, elevation towards the city [C.A.A.]
8. Währingerstrasse station, platform level plan, street level plan [C.A.A.]
9. Währingerstrasse station, sections [C.A.A.]
10. Nussdorferstrasse station [photo: M.S.]

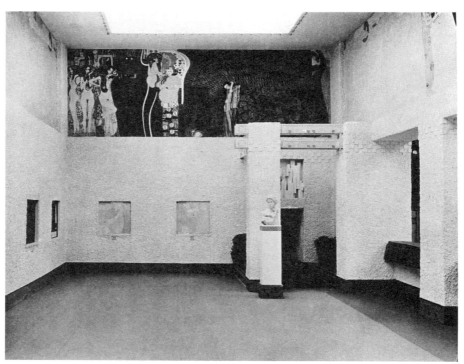

With the "Temple for the Arts" Olbrich created a key edifice not only for the history of Viennese architecture. Its synthesis of archaic and modern elements, the intense concentration of typological and symbolic references, the bold contrast between the pseudo-sacred entrance under the dome, made of gold-plated wrought-iron laurels, and the sober functionality of the exhibition tract scandalized his contemporaries. The ground plan and front view were developed from the cross shape of the vestibule, the exhibition hall itself was designed as a neutral shell, evenly distributing natural light throughout the edifice. The exhibitions organized here were integrated in varying interiors combining the exhibited articles into a "Gesamtkunstwerk".

Secession
Joseph Maria Olbrich
Vienna, 1897–98

1. Left wing with Beethoven frieze by Gustav Klimt [photo: A.V.S.]
2. Secession, before 1908 [photo: A.V.S.]

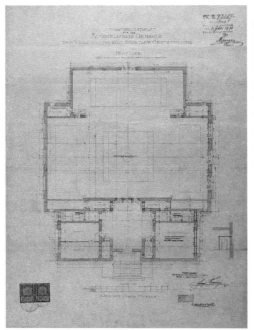

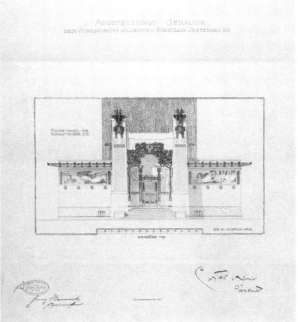

5

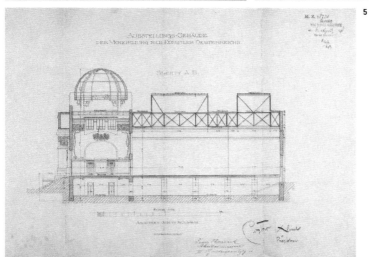

3. Plan, final design [photo: A.V.S.]
4. Main facade, entrance [photo: A.V.S.]
5. Longitudinal section [photo: A.V.S.]
6. Current state [photo: M.S.]

DER·ZEIT·IHRE·KVNST·
DER·KVNST·IHRE·FREIHEIT·

VER·SACRVM·

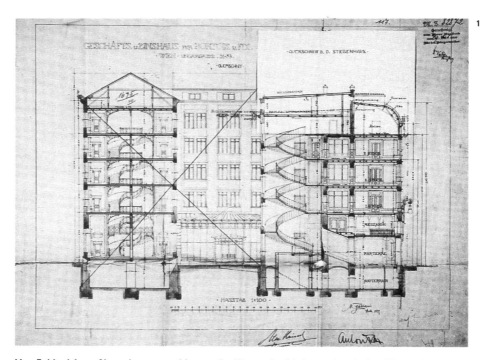

Max Fabiani from Slovenia was working on the Vienna Stadtbahn project in Otto Wagner's studio when he designed the house "Portois & Fix". With this house, commissioned by one of the most significant Viennese furniture manufacturers, Fabiani reacted to Wagner's "Majolica house" built the previous year by presenting the "even more modern solution" for the design and panelling (F. Achleitner). The panel decoration was reduced to a geometrical surface pattern while the explicit urbanity and industrial context was expressed in the two-storey basement zone through a stringent, repetitive window-door-window-door motif. The edifice served as an administrative building for the production halls behind.

1. Section [M.A.V.]
2. Facade towards the street, 1901 [photo: A.20.J.]

Apartment and commercial building Portois & Fix
Max Fabiani
Vienna, 1899–1900

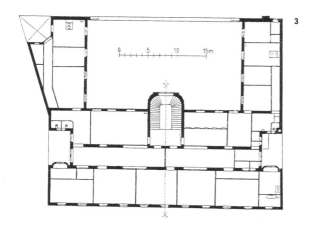

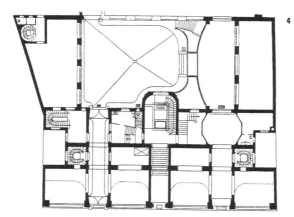

3. Apartment level plan [M.A.V.]
4. Ground floor plan [M.A.V.]
5. Detail of the facade, current state [photo: M.S.]

With the church Am Steinhof Wagner designed a prototype successfully associating ancient church-building traditions with those of the modern age. Apart from its "Byzantine" motifs, the church assembles other elements from the far past such as the Palladian windows, the antique entrance canopy, and finally the gold altar resembling a holy grave. The glass mosaics by Kolo Moser emphasize the "oriental" aura of the church. Wagner, however, developed its pioneering modernity from its use as a hospital church, which called for a sheltering atmosphere, an open view through the cruciform central room, easy access to the benches, and utmost hygiene.

1. Aerial photograph of the entire building complex [photo: A.N.L.,V.]
2. View [photo: H.M.,V.]

Church of St Leopold
Otto Wagner
Vienna, 1902–07

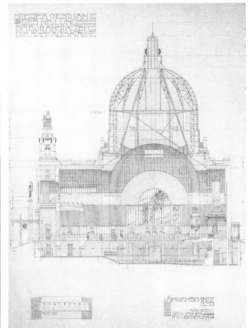

3 4

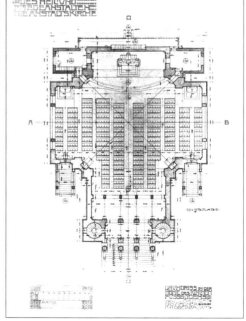

5

3. Side elevation [H.M.,V.]
4. Longitudinal section [H.M.,V.]
5. Plan [H.M.,V.]
6. Church interior [photo: M.S.]

Otto Wagner's rationalistic doctrine was translated by his students from the succession states of the Austro-Hungarian Empire into a distinct "national" modernism for various countries. After 1918, Plečnik accomplished this both on the castle overseeing Prague and in Ljubljana, his native town. The "Zacherl House" with its grid-like structure consisting of reinforced concrete supports and the treatment of the edifice's "skin" take on a typical Otto Wagner theme. The polished granite plates are supported by vertical bulbs. The house is accessed via an entree of glittering dark marble, leading to the oval staircase. Here, a trunk-like candelabrum sculpture serves as a plastic memorial to the owner who became rich in the pesticide business.

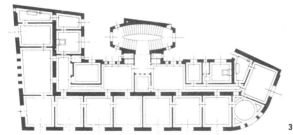

3

Zacherl House
Josef Plečnik
Vienna, 1903-05

1. Stairway [photo: M.S.]
2. Sketch [A.M.L.]
3. Upper level plan [A.M.L.]
4. From Brandstätte street [photo: M.S.]

5

5. Stairway [photo: M.S.]
6. Corner of Wildbretmarkt and Brandstätte street [photo: A.M.L.]

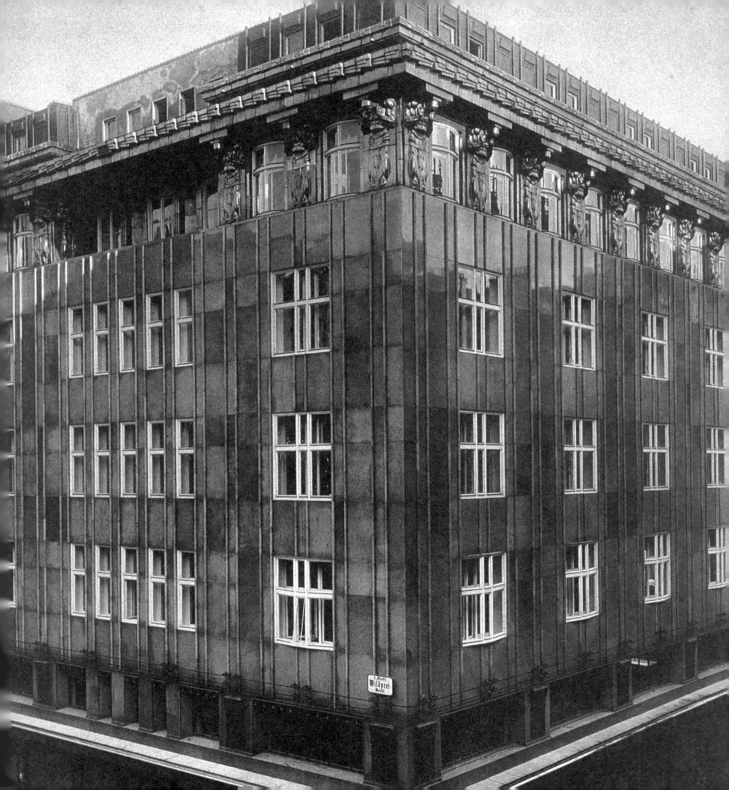

Initially conceived as a palatial Ringstrasse-style building in free neo-renaissance fashion, Wagner transformed the Austrian Post Bank building into a symbol of the modern world by applying the latest technologies and the resulting abstract formal language. Wagner systematically used the "outer skin" of the building to work with the relationship between tradition and modernism. Metal bolts fasten the panelling to the outer walls, and both the entrance canopy and the cornice sculptures are made of light metals. The highlight of this edifice, which was completed in two construction phases, is the banking hall. The consistent use of modern materials and construction methods (ventilation system) allowed Wagner to transform this basilica-like space into a shrine of technological beauty wrapped in glass on all sides - even the floor is made of glass elements.

Postal Savings Bank
Otto Wagner
Vienna, 1904

1. Competition design, site plan and perspective
2. Main entrance
[photo and drawing: A.P.S.B.,V.]

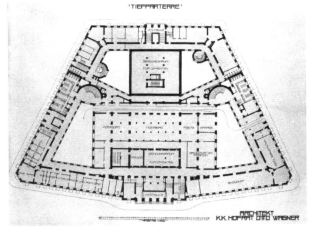

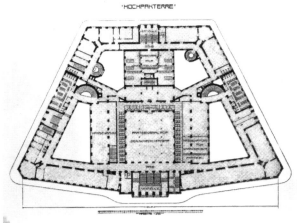

3. Longitudinal section
4. First floor plan
5. Ground floor plan
6. Banking hall
[photos and drawings: A.P.S.B.,V.]

With its "clarity of disposition, continuity of formal elaboration and especially through the extraordinary simplicity of its cubical form, the masterpiece of the cubic–geometric phase of Viennese Art Nouveau is a building which in 1904 was as pioneering as the Larkin building in Buffalo by F.L. Wright, the Scotland Street School in Glasgow by Mackintosh, and Wagner's Postal Savings Bank" (E.Sekler). The reinforced concrete edifice expressed a persistent formal language of geometry in the staircase and dining hall. Hoffmann designed the sanatorium interior, whose individual pieces rank among the most notable in furniture design of this era.
In 1926, the Wagner student Leopold Bauer added a storey to the house; it was removed again in 1995.

Sanatorium Westend
Josef Hoffmann
Purkersdorf, Lower Austria, 1904

1. From the east, after the renovation 1995 [photo: M.S.]
2. From the west, perspective
3. Entrance hall [photo: M.S.]

The fashion house "Goldman & Salatsch" was Loos's first opportunity to build a large-scale city building. In opposition to the imperial historicism of the surrounding architecture and in line with the Secession's interpretation of modern art, Loos compared his facade design to the bourgeois classicism of the Church of St Michael on the opposite side of the square. With its precious materials and formal motifs (marble and pillars), the concrete skeleton structure makes for a complex spatial arrangement of the commercial area, acquiring a representative appearance even to the outside, while the "bareness" of the simple roughcast front of the apartment floor above caused a public outcry. It was not until decades later that the "Loos house" was acknowledged epochal significance as one of the achievements mirroring the paradoxes and radical innovations of the time.

Michaeler House

Adolf Loos

Vienna, 1910

1. Elevations of the three street facades [G.C.A.G.,V.]
2. From Michaelerplatz, 1930 [photo: A.N.L.V.]

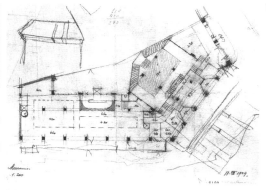

5

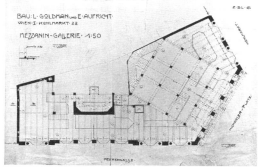

3. Ground floor sales area, stair to upper level
4. Mezzanine plan, sketch
5. Mezzanine plan
6. Mezzanine, looking towards the entrance hall
from material stockroom
[photos and drawings: G.C.A.G.,V.]

CZECH REPUBLIC

LOWER AUSTRIA

SLOVAKIA

Linz ○ **86**

St. Pölten ○

VIENNA

Vienna ○

UPPER AUSTRIA

62 64 66 72
80 82 90 92

102

GERMANY

98

Salzburg ○

70

Eisenstadt ○

Bregenz ○

STYRIA

BURGEN
LAND

HUNGARY

VORARLBERG

76 ○ Innsbruck

96

SALZBURG

Graz ○

LIECHTENSTEIN

TYROL

104

EAST TYROL

Lienz ○

CARINTHIA

SWITZERLAND

Klagenfurt ○

ITALY

SLOVENIA

Modernism and "Heimat" (1920 - 1945)

The monarchy was followed by a state in which nobody believed. In Vienna, social democracy more or less fulfilled the role of a royal protectorate during the heroic "Rotes Wien" (Red Vienna) epoch. The Karl-Marx-Hof was the new Schönbrunn Palace and Clemens Holzmeister the creator of a romantic form of expressionism. This stood in contrast to the pure reason of bourgeois modernism. Alongside Ludwig Wittgenstein's unique achievements, Josef Frank opened a new perspective, free of ideological sentiment, on the question of housing. Buildings by Ernst A. Plischke, Lois Welzenbacher and Franz Baumann were perfect examples of the commencement of a new interpretation of landscape, and the Grossglockner high-alpine road became a symbol of the new republic. Yet before the new architecture could really begin to evolve, it was put to an end first in 1934 and then finally in 1938. Structures of war were built until 1945, while 60,000 flats were made vacant for Aryans: a consequence of the criminal deportation of the Jews. During this time, Austrian architecture was designed only in exile.

The rules for a good house basically do not change. They need only to be constantly reconsidered. How should one enter the garden? How should the path to the main gate look? What shape should an anteroom be? How does one pass the cloakroom on the way from the anteroom to the living room? How is the seating arranged in relation to the door and the window? There are so many questions like these, which have to be answered, and out of them, the elements of a house are formed. This is modern architecture. JOSEF FRANK

The essential quality of a building lies in the tension between the spatial concept and function on the one hand, and the vision of an architectural sculpture and the construction on the other. This tension is what brings a building to life. Without it, one is left with either pure utilitarianism or a completely abstract architectural sculpture. ERNST A. PLISCHKE

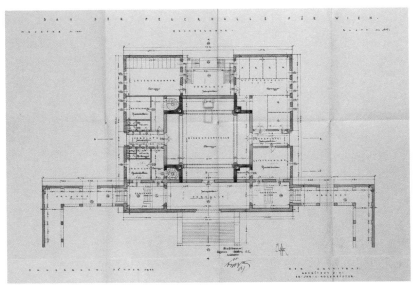

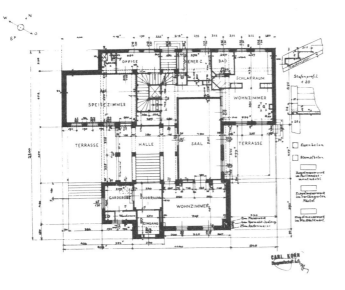

Paul Engelmann, student of Adolf Loos and secretary of Karl Kraus, was one of Wittgenstein's closest friends. Wittgenstein's sister entrusted him with the design of the residential palace. Wittgenstein himself was asked to assist in planning the details and managing construction. He was responsible for the refinement characteristic of all dimensions and details and mainly employed artificial, modern materials and new techniques: floor heating, special window and door designs made of fine iron, precast stone floors, lift, metal curtains. Wittgenstein's architecture thus resembled his philosophy in that he also drew a line between the speakable and the unspeakable, stripped the syntax of classical architecture of all its rhetoric, leading back to ground zero where it can be regarded "sub specie aeternitatis".

Wittgenstein House
Paul Engelmann
Ludwig Wittgenstein
Vienna, 1926–28

1. Hall [photo: M.S.]
2. Ground floor plan, second version, November 1926 [M.A.V.]
3. From the south [photo: M.N.]

Karl-Marx-Hof became rooted in the minds of the people as a mythical symbol of social housing projects in Vienna. This is primarily due to the symbolic power emanating from the facility's towers and gate passages at its centre, which are however merely a fraction of the 1,325 flats in the entire complex. However, the remarkable tectonic feat consists not so much in the "fortifying" signs, but in the idea that all apartments must be able to benefit equally from the large green gardens located within the three courtyards. More than anything else, the building project represents the "super block" type which was built by the social-democratic city council between 1924 and 1934. Karl Ehn was a student of Otto Wagner and remained loyal to the city council throughout all regime changes until the fifties.

Karl-Marx-Hof
Karl Ehn
Vienna, 1926-30

1. Aerial view of the entire building complex [photo: A.N.L.V.]
2. Site plan [M.A.V.]
3. From courtyard, current state, April 1998 [photo: M.S.]
4. Central wing [photo: A.N.L.,V.] pp. 68-69

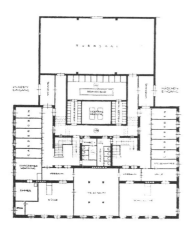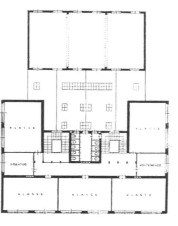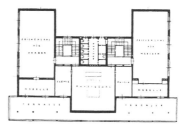

Julius Schulte ranks among those architects who, after having studied in Vienna, represented the objectives of modern art at a high level in the federal provinces. After 1910, he chiefly built schools, children's homes, workers' hostels, firefighter schools, and housing projects in Upper Austria. The originally crimson school in Ebensee reveals a regional reinterpretation of this vocation. The creative elements such as flagpoles, the loggia–like balcony running around the building, and the round windows in the uppermost floor also signal the claim to cultural progress in the institution and architecture.

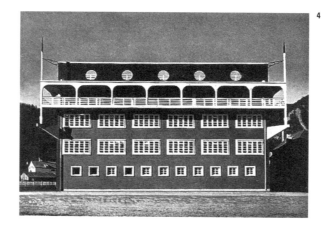

4

Ebensee Secondary School
Julius Schulte
Ebensee, Upper Austria, 1927

1. Ground floor plan
2. First floor plan
3. Third floor plan
4. Frontage [photo: Ö.B.W.1930/31]
5. Rear side with gymnasium [photo: Ö.B.W.1930/31]

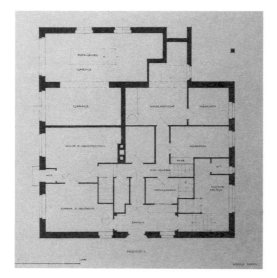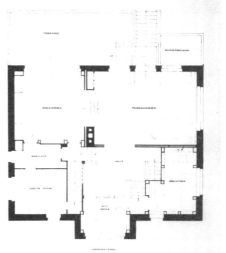

With the Moller House (and in 1930 with the Mueller House in Prague), Loos succeeded in demonstrating his "spatial plan" to perfection. This architectural concept offers an alternative to Le Corbusier's "plan libre". With it, Loos transposed conventional foundation planning into a third dimension: depending on its function and significance, each single room is connected to the others vertically and horizontally, at different heights, by short flights of stairs.

The symmetrical and nearly aversive street facade hardly explains the complex interlocking of salon, library, dining rooms, and reading rooms in the interior. Loos designed the Haus Tristan Tzara in Paris and left the local building supervision to Jacques Groag, one of the most talented architects in Vienna during the time between the two World Wars.

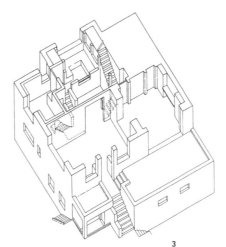

1. First floor plan
2. Ground floor plan
3. Isometric section
[drawings: G.C.A.G.,V.]
4. From street [photo: M.G., G.C.A.G.,V.]

3

Moller House
Adolf Loos
Vienna, 1927–28

5. Looking towards dining hall
6. Garden side, photograph from 1929
[photos: M.G., G.C.A.G.,V.]

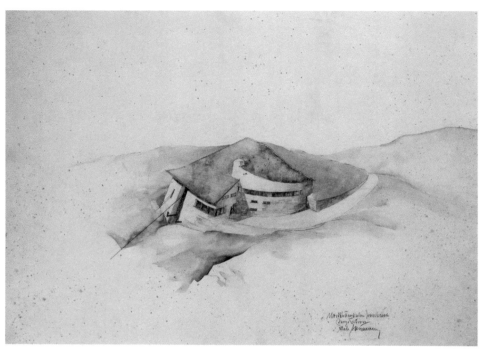

The three stations of the Nordkettenbahn (lower station Hungerburg, 863 m; middle station Seegrub, 1,905 m; mountain station Hafelekar, 2,256 m) are spectacular examples of how innovative construction can be interpreted to serve tourism in the context of modernity. Depending on the altitude, Baumann developed increasingly liberal shapes, resulting in a pitched roof for the middle station and a structure designed exclusively to harbour cable car entry and a passenger pier for the mountain station. Thus a unique aesthetic project was developed, resulting naturally from the stipulated requirements. This position of modern, non-folklorist construction for tourism was developed in the 1920s, but dismissed during the boom in the years following World War II.

Franz Baumann
Innsbruck, Tyrol, 1927–28

1. Top station Hafelekar, design [T.C.M.F.]
2. Top station [photo: F.A.]

3

4

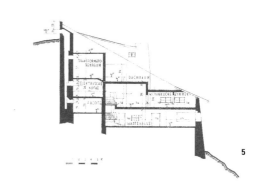

5

6 7 8

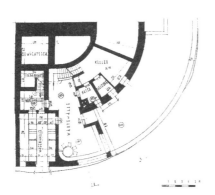  

3. Middle station [photo: Ö.B.W. 1928/29]
4. Top station Hafelekar, side elevation
5. Top station Hafelekar, section through guest rooms
6. Basement plan
7. Ground floor plan
8. Upper level plan
[drawings: T.U.I.]
9. Dining room at the top station [photo: Ö.B.W. 1928/29]

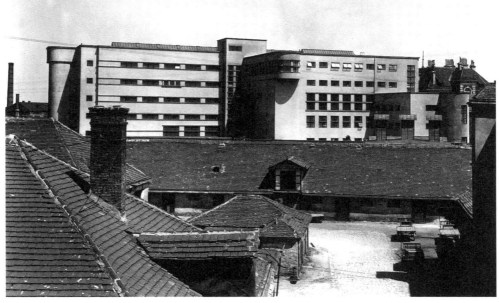

The substation represents the mood of an epoch that bravely demonstrates the achievements of a metropolis in modern industrial society caught in the throes of its social and technical making. The monumental cubes and cylinders, quadrangles and projecting "command bridges", and the complete system of "machine aesthetics", constitute a significant link between expressive and "objective" tendencies. The difficulties posed by the triangular plot of land virtually seem to have inspired this form of creativity.

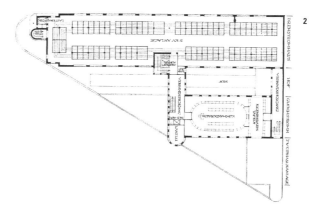

1. General view from the west [photo: A.N.L.V.]
2. Control level plan [Ö.B.W., 1931]
3. From the west, connecting passage [photo: A.N.L.V.]

Substation Favoriten
Eugen Kastner, Fritz Waage
Vienna, 1928–31

Along with the Moller House by Adolf Loos, the Beer House is the most significant creation of Viennese architecture as regards housing projects of the 1920s and '30s. The Beer House is the manifesto embodying Frank's idea of "the house as a pathway and place", further developing Loos's concept of spatial planning. The aim was to allow inhabitants to find an ambiance in harmony with their moods by means of a series of varying spatial adventures, as in a city. Around 1930, the lightness of architecture and furnishings mirrored the position of an autonomous modernity in Vienna, whose unfolding, however, was prevented by the historical caesuras of 1934 and 1938.

Beer House
Josef Frank
Oskar Wlach
Vienna, 1929-31

1. From the street
2. Garden side
[photos: M.B. 1932]

3

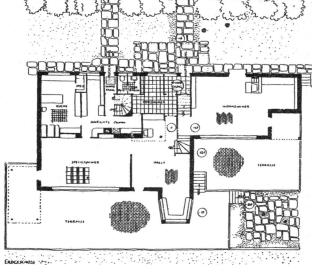

STOCKWERK

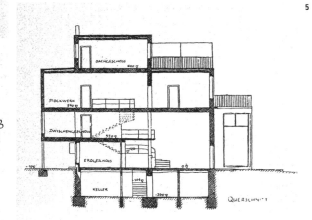

5

QUERSCHNITT

ERDGESCHOSS

4

3. Second floor plan
4. Ground floor plan
5. Section
[drawings: M.A.V.]
6. Stair towards mezzanine, music room and office
[photo: M.B. 1932]

Peter Behrens was Professor at the Vienna Academy of Fine Arts from 1921 to 1936. The "general extensions and alterations" commissioned by the "Tabakregie" company, which held a monopoly in the tobacco industry, "is one of the greatest international achievements of industrial construction in the '30s" (F. Achleitner). The business requirements stipulating uninterrupted air-conditioning with 80% humidity and continuous lighting were crucial for determining the construction technology and design to be applied. "The face of this edifice tells everyone what it is – a factory building. Similarly to the arrangement of floor after floor, working room after working room in the interior, the exterior also mirrors this horizontal rhythm" (Behrens/Popp).

After the "Anschluss" in 1938, the assistant of Behrens, Alexander Popp, turned out to be a National Socialist. He became President of the Academy of Fine Arts, and from 1939 to 1943, was chief architect of the Linzer "Hermann-Göering Works" named after their founder, today's Voest-Alpine Steel Works.

1. Power station, sketch [A.T.,L.]
2. Tobacco factory, from the southeast [photo: M.S.]

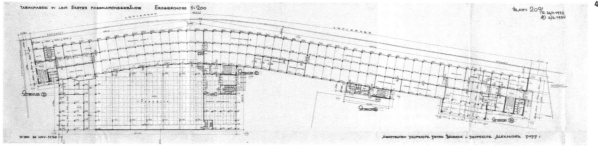

3. Tobacco factory, from the northwest with staircases in foreground [photo: A.N.L.,V.]
4. Ground floor plan [A.T.,L.]
5. Power station [photo: D.n.T.,L. 1932]

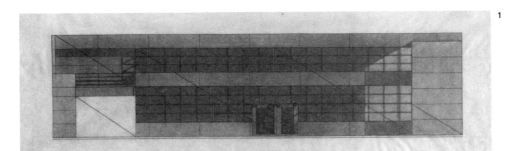

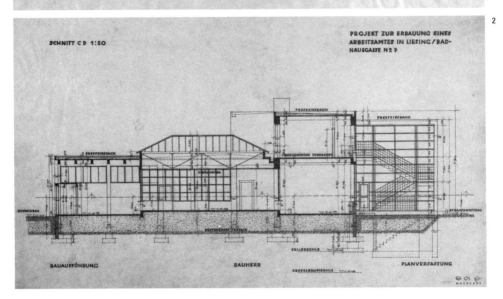

This edifice ranks among the most radical designs of Viennese modernism dating back to the years between the two World Wars. In the early 1930s, Plischke, a student of Oskar Strnad and Peter Behrens, represented the position of rational "white" modern art in Le Corbusier's sense of the concept. His first large-scale project already illustrates this idea of transparent and poetical tectonics. This gives the entire building an almost forced transparency and optical lightness and finds expression especially in the projecting glass prism of the staircase. The continuous row of windows, the organizational and technical refinement of the interior, and the subtle details of the concrete skeleton construction helped the then 28-year old architect to become the most prominent figure in Austria's architectural scene.

1. Street side facade, schematic elevation of proportion system
2. Section
3. Street side facade and forecourt
[photos and drawings: U.F.A.,V.]

Liesing Labour Office
Ernst Anton Plischke
Vienna, 1930–32

Inspired by predecessors in Stuttgart/Weissenhof (1927) and Breslau (1929), this illustrative Viennese complex also implied criticism of "Red Vienna's", i.e. socialist, monumental housing program. Josef Frank assumed the project's overall management and also chose the architects to be invited. The 70 houses were equipped with model interiors in 1932 and opened to the public. They were meant to introduce a range of sample, modern house models for future housing complexes. Frank's aim was – in contrast to the Weissenhof project – not to propagate a new ideology, but to demonstrate the diversity of spatial and functional solutions that could be created even with the reduced formal and economical means of modern building: a pluralism of typified – not standardized – housing without pathos.

Werkbundsiedlung
Josef Frank (project leader)
Vienna, 1930–32

1. General view [photo: M.G.]
2. Site plan [M.A.V.]

2

3. Poster of the Wiener Werkbundsiedlung exhibition, 1932
4. Garden side of the buildings by Lurçat und Hoffmann
5. "Anger": buildings by Guevrekian, Rietveld, Wachberger, W. Loos, Bieber and Niedermoser
[photos: U.A.A.,V.]

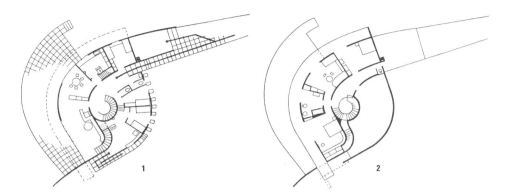

Welzenbacher had his origins in the Munich School and contributed powerful, radiating poetry to the Austrian avant-garde of the 1920s to '50s. He himself named three design priorities of construction in landscapes: close relationship to the surroundings, functionality, and the representation of the inhabitants' "spirit of life". "Modern man wishes to have his need for nature and feeling for the natural environment expressed in the home. Nature, not as imitation around the house, but the house itself as an organism breathing the sun, turning its organs to face the day, relaxed in the configuration of the floor plan, with generous views of the landscape, as though the interface to all that beauty outside was raised to become a creature itself..." (Lois Welzenbacher).

Heyrovsky House
Lois Welzenbacher
Zell am See, Salzburg, 1932

1. Ground floor
2. Upper level plan
[Drawings: A.F.A.]
3. From the southwest [photo: T.C.M.F.]
4. From the north [photo: A.D.S.]
5. Overlooking the lake from the roof [photo: A.D.S.]

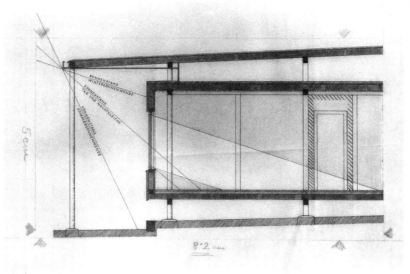

The house on the banks of the Attersee ranks among those rare examples where an inseparable synthesis between architecture and nature was created.

E.A. Plischke: "The building is a simple wooden skeleton. In order to ensure efficient floor heating, the floor is made of a solid slab of closely fitted tree logs. There is an insulating air pocket between the ceiling and the rafters. The continuous window wall stands as an autonomous element in front of the skeleton construction. The overhanging roof protects the window against the midday summer sun, but allows the winter sun to enter. In order to create harmony between the contour of the house and the forest beyond, the outline was laid with timber battens on site during the design phase. At the same time, the height of the windows was determined using this structure as framework for the view."

Gamerith House
Ernst Anton Plischke
Seewalchen, Upper Austria, 1933-34

1. Section through details, study of the incidence of sunlight
2. General view
[photo and drawing: U.F.A.,V.]

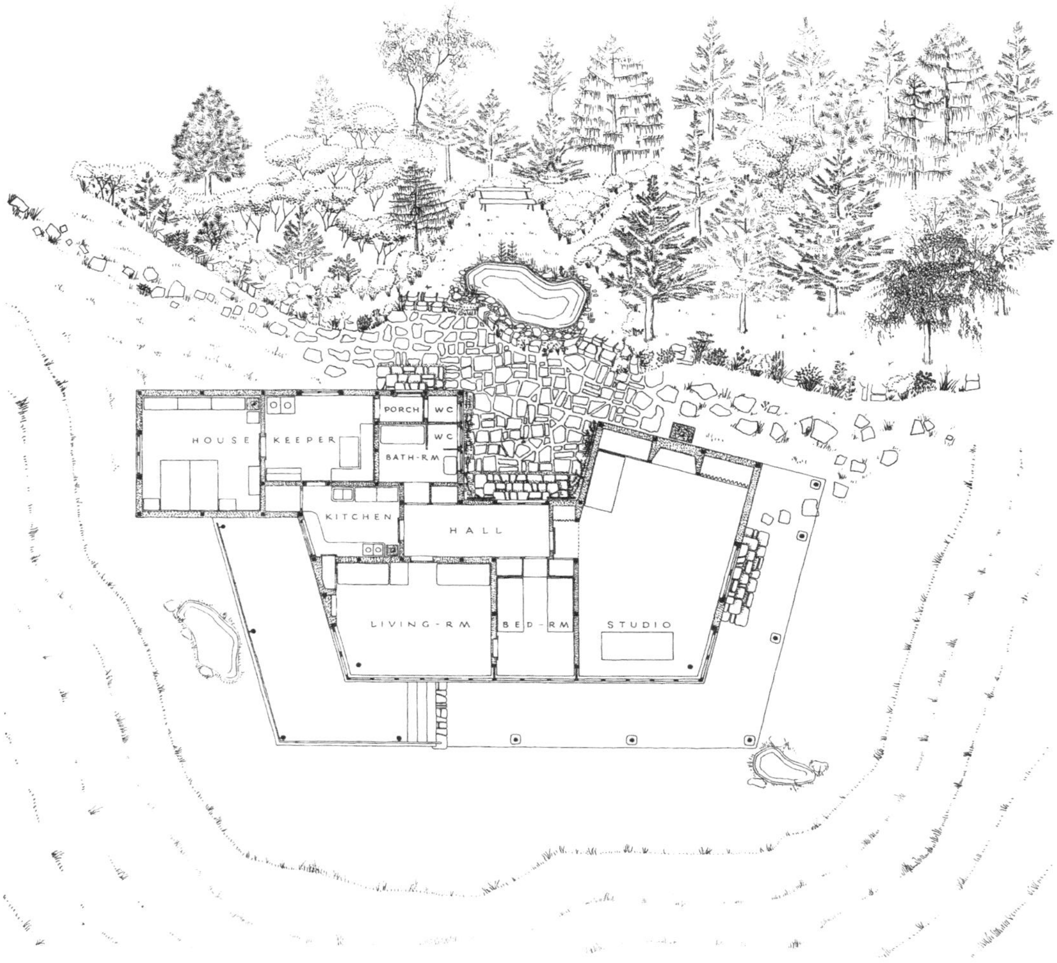
HOUSE KEEPER
PORCH
WC
WC
BATH-RM
KITCHEN
HALL
LIVING-RM
BED-RM
STUDIO

3

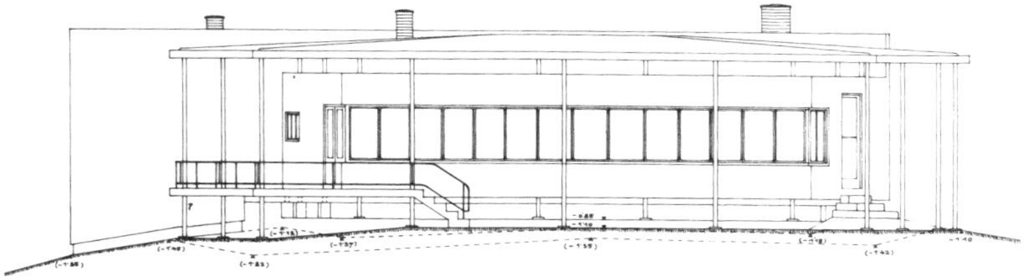

4

3. Plan
4. Main elevation
5. Lake view from the terrace
[photo and drawings: U.F.A.,V.]

1

2 3

In Peter Behrens's school at the Vienna Academy, Steineder developed his original
mode of expression and modernity, which he applied to create noteworthy buildings
– especially for the order of the school nuns in Upper Austria – in the late 1920s and
early '30s. The girls' secondary school in Attnang–Puchheim is one of his greatest
typological accomplishments. Four classrooms are arranged on two sides of a central
cruciform hall. The staircase is a tectonic element of its own, which provides entry
to the hall as to a public square. The design of details and the attention carefully paid
to pattern and surfaces are essential for the tectonic quality of the building. The floor
ornament in the hall thus retraces the structure of the house and its arrangement.

Girls' Secondary School
Hans Steineder
Attnang Puchheim,
Upper Austria, 1934–35

1. Perspective with stairway [L.S.]
2. Main entrance elevation [L.S.]
3. Rear elevation [L.S.]
4. Main face [photo: M.S.]

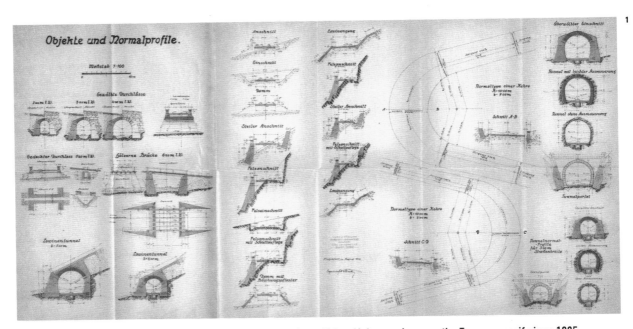

The civil engineer Franz Wallack had been promoting plans for a 48 km Alpine road across the Tauern massif since 1925. When deciding where to route the road, the experienced mountaineer was intent on avoiding the locations where several metres of snow do not melt before summer begins. At the same time, he wanted as few bends as possible.

Dead-end roads were built to access attractive view points for tourists: they lead to the Franz-Joseph point, 2363 m, at the foot of which the Pasterze, Austria's largest glacier, spreads out, and to the Edelweiss Peak, 2577 m, with a panorama view of numerous other peaks. As a landscape sensation of national significance and with the annual royal leg of the Austria cycling race, the Grossglockner Alpine road has become the country's touristic icon.

Grossglockner Alpine Road
Franz Wallack
Salzburg/Carinthia, 1930–35

1. Construction details of the tunnels and roads [G.H.AG,S.]
2. Roads in the open country [photo: G.H.AG,S.]
3. Marked-out routes inbetween the villages Fuschl
and Heiligenblut [A.N.L.,V.]

CZECH REPUBLIC

LOWER AUSTRIA

SLOVAKIA

Linz o **120 130**

St. Pölten o

Vienna o VIENNA

UPPER AUSTRIA

108 110 112 114
122 124 126
128 138
140 144

118

o Eisenstadt

134
Salzburg o

GERMANY

STYRIA

BURGEN
LAND

HUNGARY

Bregenz
o

o Innsbruck

SALZBURG

o Graz

VORARLBERG

142

TYROL

132

o

LIECHTENSTEIN

EAST TYROL

CARINTHIA

Lienz o

SWITZERLAND

Klagenfurt o

ITALY

SLOVENIA

Displacement and Progress (1945 - 1975)

A long and difficult educational process was necessary to overcome the long-term effects of Nazi ideology. The rediscovery of mostly exiled, or emigrated Austrian modernism, was part of an initial involvement in international developments enabling post-war Austrian architecture to go its own way. Public and church building projects offered the first opportunities for new architecture. The Wiener Stadthalle (Sports Hall) by Roland Rainer became the most important building in the early days. The euphoria of progress followed on from these first unique technological and typological achievements. This in turn merged into the utopias of the Viennese and Graz avant-garde of the sixties, which came to be known as the "Austrian phenomenon." An innovative, critical approach to historical building fabric also began at a very early stage in Austria, opening a new perspective that went beyond functionalism and dealt with symbolic and emotional aspects of architecture.

If we concentrate on the few individual achievements after 1945, then we must conclude that the major representative projects of the post-war generation have failed. The following generation of young architects had little to learn from their predecessors. It was up to their own initiative to re-establish contact with Austrian and international tradition.
FRIEDRICH ACHLEITNER

Cities are made for people and not the other way around, as would often appear to be the case in the rebuilding of the cities. We have just survived a period in which people's lives were "cheap." Perhaps it is no coincidence that urban planning during this time placed more emphasis on technology, design, concept and symbolic effect than on people's needs. If in the future, people's lives are no longer to be so "cheap," then it will also be a requirement of cities that they are built right down to the last detail according to the needs and standards of people.
ROLAND RAINER

Everything is architecture.
HANS HOLLEIN

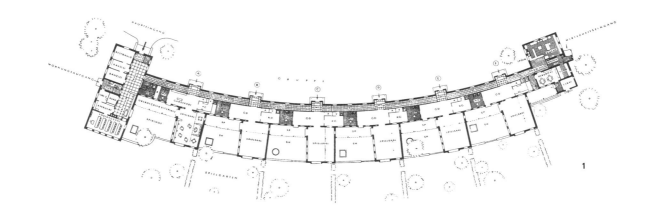

1

A student of Heinrich Tessenow, active in Frankfurt until 1936, and advocate of a moderate, detail-oriented functionalism, Schuster became the most influential figure of Vienna's post-war reconstruction period after 1945. The composition of irregularity and restrained order in the kindergarten shows how carefully Schuster designed the entire complex for physically and mentally handicapped children. "So that the window casements do not open into the room where they might be in the way, as with the tables near the windows in the dining hall, sliding windows have been installed. These are, however, divided by bars in the childrens' recreation rooms to avoid the destruction of the rooms' cosy effect with large windows."

2

Schweizerspende
Kindergarten
Franz Schuster
Vienna, 1948-49

1. Ground floor plan
2. Play room
3. From the south
[photos and drawing: U.A.A.,V.]

The Gänsehäufel is a significant link between the socialist nudist culture of "Red Vienna" and liberated modernity after World War II. With a beach big enough to cater for 30,000 persons, the architects intended "to avoid as far as possible the impression of a monster lake, which explains the arrangement of middle and inner courts that constitute spatial dividers, render the entire complex more intimate while facilitating orientation. This explains the lack of representative, axial clusters of buildings and the relaxed arrangement ... Visitors - stressed and in need of relaxation on arrival - should not be welcomed by some stiff symmetry but by a natural yet well-tended garden, in which the buildings are nicely arranged next to each other, but without pathos, for which there is no reason."

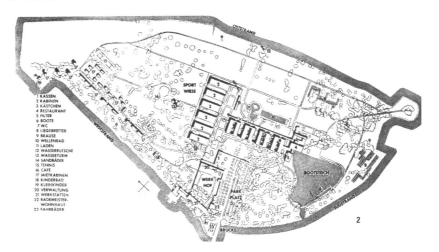

Gänsehäufel
Beach Facility

Max Fellerer
Eugen Wörle
Vienna, 1948–50

1. Courtyard with changing rooms
2. Site plan [L.W.]
3. Mushroom-shaped terrace
[photos: L.C.]

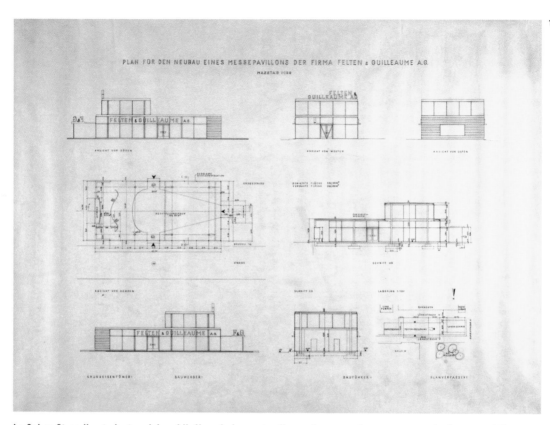

As Oskar Strnad's student and Josef Hoffman's long-standing colleague, whose successor he became at the School for Arts and Industry in 1935, Oswald Haerdtl represented the continuity of Vienna's modern art, bridging the caesura of the Second World War. His most brilliant achievements were the glazed Austrian pavilions for the World Fair in Brussels in 1935 and in Paris in 1937. The pavilion on the Vienna Fairgrounds, a canopy-like, filigree contrivance enfolded in a sheath of glass, ranks among the most liberal and consistent achievements of the optimistic reconstruction phase of the '50s. It was however typical for the entire cultural situation that this attitude was restricted to temporary architecture for exhibitions and hardly became popular anywhere else.

1. Proposal plan [L.H., AZW.]
2. From the southwest [photo: L.C.]

**Fair pavilion
Felten & Guilleaume**
Oswald Haerdtl
Vienna, 1951–53

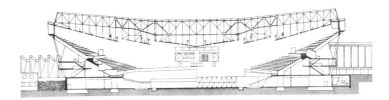

The "Wiener Stadthalle" complex came to be a centre of events, sports and training halls in a process that started in 1952 and involved several construction phases. The central hall measuring 100 x 100 m was erected between 1954 and 1958 and was intended for an audience of 15,000 to 20,000. Its roof sweeps down towards the middle, reproducing the movement of the tribunes. The idea was further pursued in the three performance and training halls with a visible armoured steel structure. The indoor swimming pool, whose construction began 1971, reveals not only all steel supports but also all aerial and electric lines as equal elements in terms of the constructive language of modern architecture. In 1994 an additional exhibition and event hall with bare steel framework and aerial lines followed.

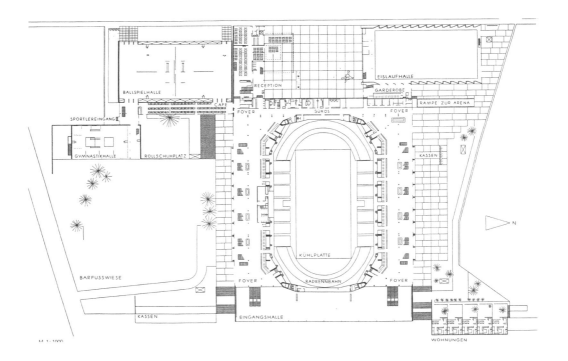

Sports Hall
Roland Rainer
Vienna, 1952–58, 1971–74, 1994

1. Section through main hall [A.R.]
2. Plan without swimming pool [A.R.]
3. Main hall [photo: L.C.]

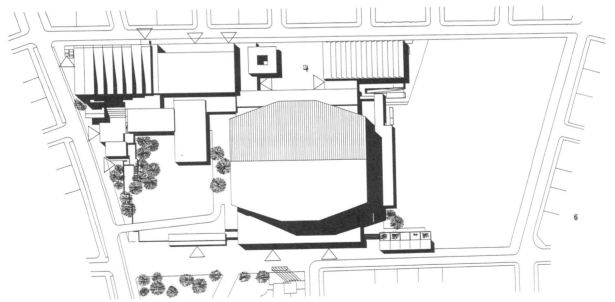

6

4. Main hall, interior [photo: F.H.]
5. Indoor swimming pool, stair towards grandstand [photo: A.R.]
6. Site plan with swimming pool [A.R.]
7. Indoor swimming pool with E-hall in foreground [photo: A.R.]

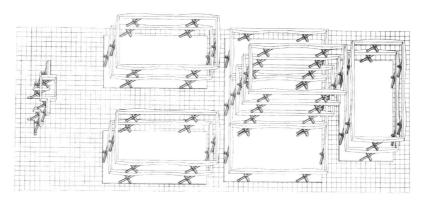

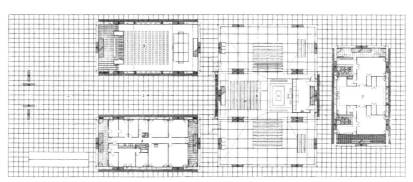

The pastoral counselling area plays a special role in the history of Austrian church architecture. It is the theme of the constructivist school, strongly influenced by Konrad Wachsmann, and a symbol for church renewal, which is characterized by a tendency towards secularization, demystification, and desymbolization in sacred buildings. The edifice follows the Wachsmann doctrine in that it is developed from a single bearing element, the x-support. Another principle of the centre is the strict separation of "the skeleton and the skin". The longitudinal beams of the framework are sculptured, in analogy to the momentary impression, and the bearing walls also communicate an inner progression of strength and, in an expressive way, represent the whole constructive achievement.

Pastoral Counselling Centre Ennsleiten

Arbeitsgruppe 4 [Wilhelm Holzbauer, Friedrich Kurrent, Johannes Spalt] and Johann Georg Gsteu
Steyr, Upper Austria, 1958–61

1. Axonometric of the structure, 1960 [A.A.]
2. Entire building complex, floor plan [A.A.]
3. Construction phase [photo: K.M.]

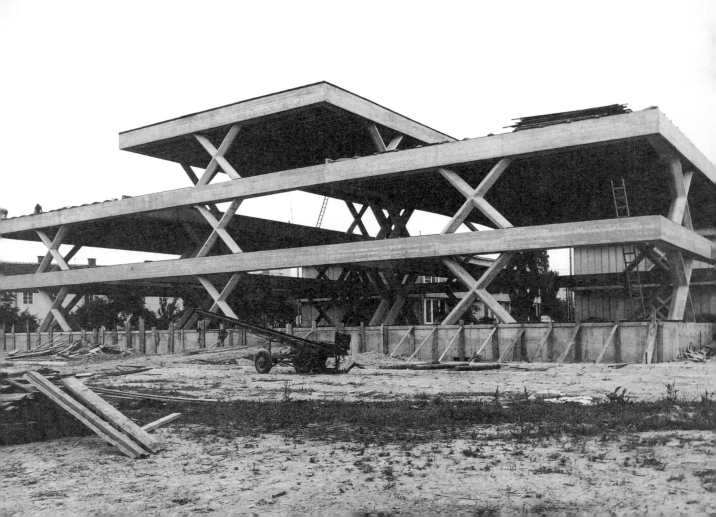

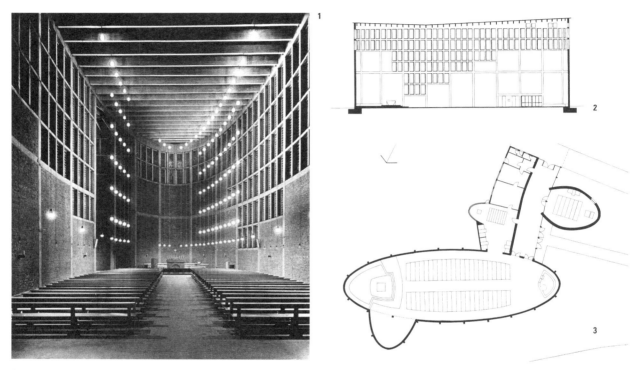

1
2
3

Rudolf Schwarz was very much aware of the baroque tradition characterizing Linz and its surroundings when building the Church of St Therese. He noted in his plans, "the floor plan of the church is very simple. It has the shape of a rather elongated egg with an altar located in the front bay. The baptismal area is located at the rear. The area is embraced by an elliptic circle drawn from the altar to project beyond the church community, finding its way back from the apogee at the rear of the church. The apse of the altar reaches beyond the people, giving shape to another bay. The front church nave divides into a lateral nave, admitting an inflow from the small apse, which opens to the altar."

Church of St Therese
Rudolf Schwarz
Linz, Upper Austria, 1958-62

1. Church, interior
2. Section
3. Plan
4. From the northeast
[photos: E.W.]

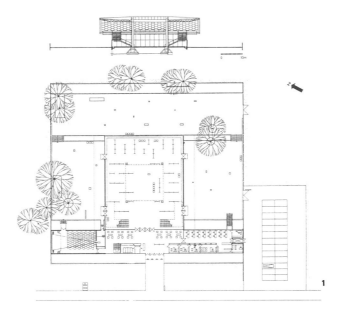

1

Originally, the steel skeleton construction was erected to serve as the Austrian pavilion at the World Fair in Brussels (1958), the square taking the shape of a courtyard between the pylons and the ground floor of a roofed clearance. Only after being rebuilt in the Vienna Schweizergarten – originally intended as temporary, it has in the meantime moved to the Museum for Modern Art of the 20th Century – was the courtyard covered and the ground floor glazed. This now embraces three courtyards for plastic sculptures, affording the museum additional surrounding space in the exhibition zone that can be used for specific purposes. As regards architecture, the building with its puristic concept is one of Austria's promises of the late fifties, which announce a link-up with international standards.

2

Museum of the 20th Century
Karl Schwanzer
Vienna, 1959–62

1. Section, ground floor plan
2. From Schweizergarten park
3. Load-bearing structure
[photos and drawings: M.20 C.,V.]

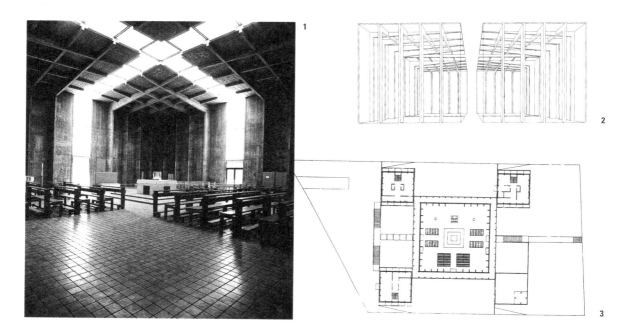

1

2

3

The project was born from a belief in the power of geometry and modular order, which brings into relation all elements, from volume to the smallest detail. The dimensions are taken from the distance between supports, which measures 180 cm; the church design and the entire complex, however, is based on the Palladian spatial volume of 1:1:1. The severity of the church interior also applies to the design of the building exterior, which extends the principle of geometrical classification to include four functions (volumes) parish court, sacristy, parish hall, and bulwark for the bell headstock (as contrasting empty space). The layering of two design principles (typos and topos, order and coincidence) produces surprising spatial diversity, which can be experienced when ambling through the premises.

Counselling Centre Baumgarten
Johann Georg Gsteu
Vienna, 1960–65

1. Church, interior [photo: F.H.]
2. Structure diagram [A.Gs.]
3. Site plan [A.Gs.]
4. General view [photo: M.S.]

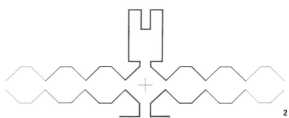
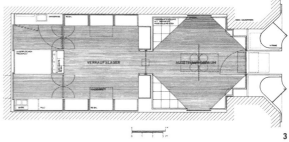

In a time when the technology craze held sway, Hollein's candle shop not only displayed a system of aesthetics based on the tools and symbols used in space flight, but with the shop design, and especially the gateway, he also revolutionized the rituals and conventions of buying and selling. A gateway made of aluminum, which gives the impression of being locked, triggers associations to candles and their candlelight as well as to key holes. The entrance has two windows at eye level that reveal the shop interior to those approaching from two sides. The visitor enters an octagonal showroom, which is expanded to infinity in the transverse axis by alternating mirror reflections.

1. Sales room [photo: F.H.]
2. Schematic drawing of a typical floor plan analysing the mirror effects [A.A.]
3. Plan [A.A.]
4. Facade [photo: F.H.]

Candle Shop Retti
Hans Hollein
Vienna, 1964–65

The church dedicated to the Holy Trinity was built to manifest Fritz Wotruba's sculptural concepts. As a kind of spatial sculpture, the layering of concrete cubes reflects the artist's ideas in spite of varying dimensions and materials. The architect Fritz G. Mayr was in charge of translating the model into actual construction. A point of conflict remains perceivable in the roofing of the concrete cubes. Achleitner: "The ceiling, which was simply placed on top, seems like the makeshift covering of a group of sculptures. As a result, the church should not have any ceiling and glazing, it should actually be a large, walkable sculpture placed into the landscape."

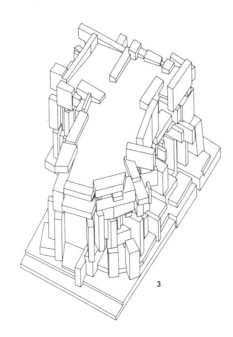

Dreifaltigkeit Church
Fritz Wotruba
Fritz G. Mayr
Vienna, 1965–76

1. From the northeast [photo: M.S.]
2. Sketch [A.F.W.]
3. Axonometric [A.F.W.]
4. Entrance [photo: M.S.]

The following aims were set, based on the ideas and concepts of the garden city movement:
an experiment with the use of minimum plot dimensions for compacted low-profile buildings,
extremely austere development by a network of narrow, lightly paved footpaths (cars in
underground garages, car parks at the outer periphery), passive use of solar energy by facing
the building complex toward the sun and a water heating system operated by sun collectors.
The concept also provided the following services: adding secluded private outside quarters
and garden courtyards enclosed by walls to the inner rooms and the erection of small-scale
elements while preserving natural and man-made green spaces. The infrastructure includes
kindergartens, several schools, shops, and a church.

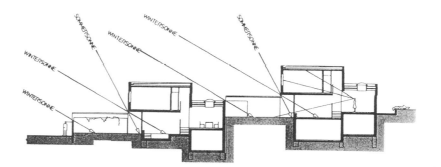

Garden City
Roland Rainer
Puchenau near Linz,
Upper Austria, 1963–95

1. Exterior with lake [photo: A.R.]
2. Section, study of the incidence of light [A.A.]
3. Aerial view of the entire building complex [photo: A.R.]

The unique spatial impression of the Felsenbad pool results from the ingenious fashion in which topographical difficulties were overcome. Since the location of the outside pool had been decided, the basin for the indoor swimming pool was dynamited into the rock. This incursion created a specially accentuated reference between indoors and outdoors.

This impression was further emphasized by the decision to leave the natural rock visible. Garstenauer limited the use of materials to rock and concrete and to wood and glass in the interior. According to Friedrich Achleitner the man-made rock pool is "a successful attempt to cover a place, to make visible its topographical features without endeavouring to interpret."

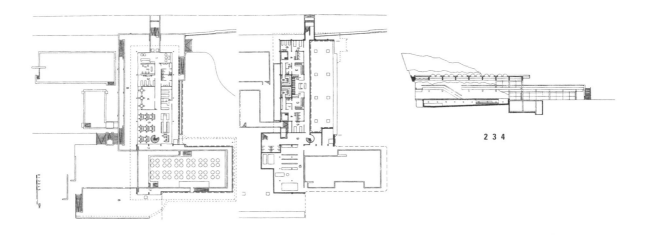

2 3 4

Felsenbad
Gerhard Garstenauer
Badgastein, Salzburg, 1967–68

1. Outdoor pool with indoor pool beyond
2-3. Plans
4. Section
5. General view
[photos and drawings: A.G.]

The ORF (Austrian Broadcasting Corporation) studios in Linz, Salzburg, Innsbruck and Dornbirn constitute an organizational and tectonic system that can be adapted to different topographical situations in keeping with vital functions and uniform elements. The cyclical organization of the complex allows all sectors to circle around a round hall and to expand into the peripheral areas. The tectonics of the provincial studios represent a "late functionalist" phase, in which technological functionalism turns itself into a theme of aesthetic representation. Gustav Peichl emphasizes this dimension of self-portrayal by means of well-calculated decisions, such as painting the concrete elements metallic silver so that they come to present a kind of alienation in themselves.

Provincial ORF Studio
Gustav Peichl
Salzburg, 1968–72

1. ORF radio station in Graz, hall [photo: A.P.]
2. Isometric
3. Salzburg radio station looking towards the castle
[photo: A.P.] pp. 136–137

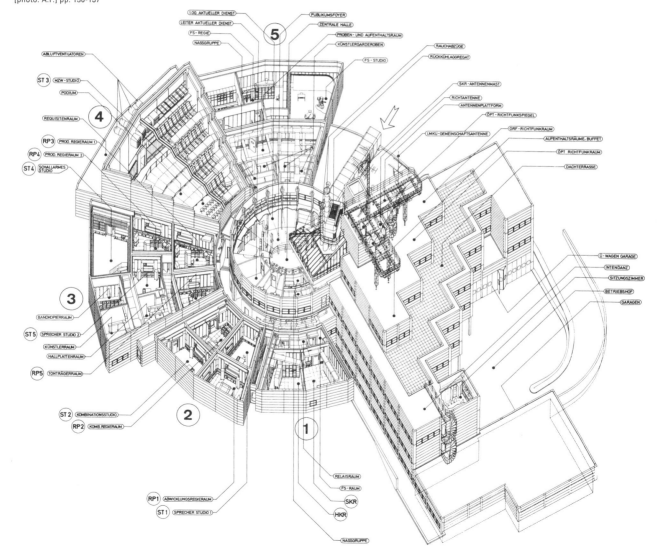

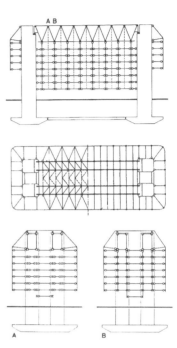

The Juridicum, Vienna's law school, is perhaps the last modern large-scale construction project in Vienna's city centre. The aim was to accommodate an extensive programme in the existing volume of the Ringstrasse blocks. The ground floor was to become a large public zone, the streets were to flow through the house as a "covered square". For the sake of easier access and to reduce the number of staircases and lifts, the auditoria were moved into the basement directly under the square. Many factors advocated the idea of suspending the entire edifice from a recessed top floor, from four steel frames to span 52 metres downwards. After many delays the building was completed and met with criticism due to the technologic investment, the extreme provocation of the situation, and its solitariness within its surroundings.

Juridicum
Ernst Hiesmayr
Vienna, 1968–84

1. Interior, ground floor and mezzanine [photo: A.H.]
2. Structure diagram
3. General view [photo: P.W.]

The complex is interesting for two reasons. First, because of the sociological and educational concept the city government had developed to house foster children. Second, because of the architectural forms determined by city planning. Thus the complex consists not only of five quadruplexes, each with room for a family with ten children, plus youth club, but also includes swimming pool, theatre, gym, restaurant, and other services (petting zoo etc.), all of which also have the purpose of attracting the public at large. The intricate room construction is organized along the street linearity and the dwellings face a large park towards the southwest.

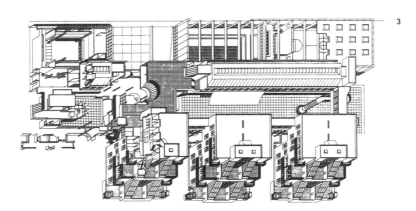

A City for Children
Anton Schweighofer
Vienna, 1969-74

1. From the east
2. South view of a dwelling unit
3. Axonometric
4. Looking at the dwellings from the southeast
[photos: M.S.]

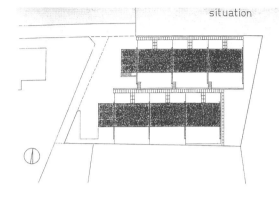

situation

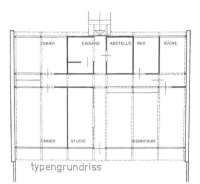

| ZIMMER | EINGANG | ABSTELLR. | BAD | KÜCHE |
| ZIMMER | STUDIO | | WOHNRAUM | |

typengrundriss

Ruhwiesen, a highly economical, tectonic wooden construction, was Austria's first housing project to be carried out directly by a cooperative of owners, whose members themselves assisted in construction. Brick walls separate the houses from each other. The remaining outer walls and the roof are made of wood. The rooms to the south are completely glazed in order to save energy, and they lie lower than the closed northern side. The design of the ground floor, the construction method, and the facade arrangement mirror Rudolf Wäger's superb economy and efficiency that wish to speak only in terms of pure and simple tectonics and for this reason have become architecture.

Ruhwiesen Housing Project
Rudolf Wäger
Schlins, Vorarlberg, 1971–73

1. Site plan, floor plans showing typical floor plan
2. Living room
3. Garden side
4. General view
[photos: R.W.]

1

A historical corner building attractively dominates the Floridsdorfer Spitz and represents the "starting point" of the new branch office building. As an equal element among the existing stock of buildings, the height of the new lateral wing is gradually reduced, agreeing both with the shape of the plot and the statical requirement of diminishing clearance above the banking hall. The open gallery behind the metal–glass facade touches on the old stock of buildings, whose structure, however, remains intact. Thus a new complete entity is created, which finds sublime, integral expression especially from the building interior. At a time when in other parts of Europe only a handful of art historians and monument conservationists had assumed a positive attitude to historicism, the architects successfully found a pioneering way to express contemporary architecture within a historical context.

2

Zentralsparkasse Bank
Floridsdorf Branch Office
Johannes Spalt
Friedrich Kurrent
Vienna, 1970–74

1. Looking from the gallery towards the banking hall
2. Section and plan
3. General exterior view
[photos: M.S.]

Spectrum of the Present
from 1975 onwards

The Panorama

The Beautiful Landscape

The Historical Location

Public Housing

[2]

CZECH REPUBLIC

LOWER AUSTRIA

SLOVAKIA

148 150 170
172 194 VIENNA
Linz ○ **184**

St. Pölten ○ **186** Vienna ○
190 **176**

160

UPPER AUSTRIA

158

Eisenstadt ○

Salzburg ○ **182**
GERMANY **178**

Bregenz ○
180 STYRIA BURGEN
LAND HUNGARY

VORARLBERG ○ Innsbruck SALZBURG

152 ○ Graz
164

TYROL

LIECHTENSTEIN

EAST TYROL
Lienz ○ CARINTHIA

SWITZERLAND **154** Klagenfurt ○

ITALY

SLOVENIA

Around the middle of the seventies, there was an increasing consolidation of regional priorities. The "Graz School" and the "Vorarlberger Baukünstler" became diametrically opposed, assuming an organic-expressive position on the one hand, and a structurally efficient refinement on the other. However, common to both groups was a willingness to become involved in residential housing. In the eighties, a major reform in urban planning took place in Salzburg. The "design advisory board" helped the city to new-found recognition through outstanding examples of internationally significant architecture. Vienna's "little architecture" concept initially began to evolve more or less underground through lavish shop and pub designs and until the mid-eighties, government policy also made the realization of larger projects possible. In Austria in the nineties, architecture exhibits great diversity and vigorous contrasts in creative achievement.

The idea of democracy evolved from the city. It was the cities, which preserved and passed this idea from one generation to the next for thousands of years. Will we witness the tragedy of the destruction of the city? Or does the appearance of our cities merely expose a society, which has not yet resolved to pursue the path of democracy fully? JOHANNES VOGGENHUBER

We will also have to acknowledge that in this country a new form of architecture exists. It assumes, through its social status, more a position of insurgency, created by architects, who, in Austria, most certainly don't receive any royal treatment. These are not only architects who are registered and employed abroad, on the contrary, there exists a much broader platform for productive, critical dialogue and quality of design.
FRIEDRICH ACHLEITNER

Architecture has to burn.
COOP HIMMELB(L)AU

Architecture is background.
HERMANN CZECH

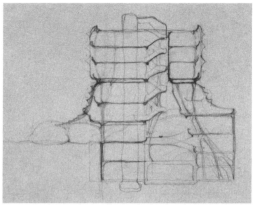

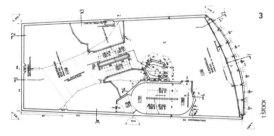

The present branch of Bank Austria in Favoriten (a district of Vienna) is the most significant structure of the "Graz School" in its early phase. Without the architecture's tense, nervous expressiveness and its pulsating language of forms, one would be compelled to call it an example of exaggerated functionalism, because each detail, each construction, each element is born of its function: thus a barren technology has been developed which comprises biomorphic metaphors – bones, tendons, skin, scales, ducts, blood vessels – all of which, however, not only demonstrate their function in a rational manner, but also show an irrational, closed, aesthetic world with its own logic and dynamics. Domenig searches for an individual, tense emotionality, which purposely goes to extremes and risks everything.

1. Facade towards the street
2. Sketched section
3. First floor plan
4. Facade towards the courtyard
[photos: A.D.]

Zentralsparkasse Bank
Favoriten Branch
Günther Domenig
Vienna, 1975-79

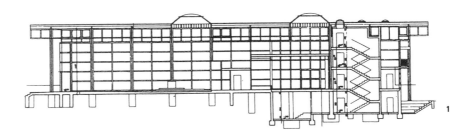

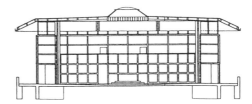

The typology of stretched farmhouses in the Alpine foothills and the rich tradition of framework construction technology in combination with their transformation into a new application and the Viennese refinement, bring forth a tectonically diverse, vivid structure, which emanates through the huge roof umbrella serenity and seclusion without slipping off into the rural or even regional. The "triad" comprising the structural framework, skin and light is a product of long spatial experience. The area surrounding the church is also "classical" in the modern sense of the term: the forecourt, the walls, the podium, which reveal the distinctive traits of the building with every ambling step. Here, Herbert Boeckl's triptych has found a dignified exhibition site.

Salvador Church
Johannes Spalt
Vienna, 1976-79

1. Longitudinal section
2. Church, interior
3. Cross section
4. From the southeast
[photos: M.S.]

The entire complex consists of three parabolic glass roofs with varying climate zones that are diagonally misaligned and a prismatic glass element with a sloping roof. This part of the building serves research and cultivation purposes. The greenhouses are open to the public and connected by runways and bridges. The light-weight construction made of aluminum allows a maximum of light to enter. A water heating system is integrated into the pipes of the supporting framework. The cooling system is made up of a valve system able to emit microscopical fog. The concave and pulvinate, double-layered acrylic glass elements define the building's tectonic expression, which differs from conventional greenhouse construction and tends to appear as a body of dual tension.

1. Aerial view
2. Tropical pavilion, interior with bridge
[photos: H.G.T.]

**Institute of Botany
Greenhouses**
Volker Giencke
Graz, Styria, 1982–93

For more than 20 years, Günther Domenig has been working with this place, which is closely linked to his childhood days. To this day the stone house at the banks of the Ossiacher Lake remains an unfinished project. The house is intended to resemble a piled up hill from which rocks break out, bare rocks without any vegetation, rocks that reveal the stone. Domenig sees this as an "attempt, perhaps, to find a way back to a type of home architecture that does not sweep away our traces". As the concentration and monument of his tectonic ideas, the stone house explains itself and the world and is communication and legacy at the same time: "I have come to my limits in every respect, here we will see what I am actually able to do in architecture." (Günther Domenig)

1. From the south
2. Floating stone 1
[photos: G.v.B.]

Stone House
Günther Domenig
Steindorf, Carinthia, as of 1986

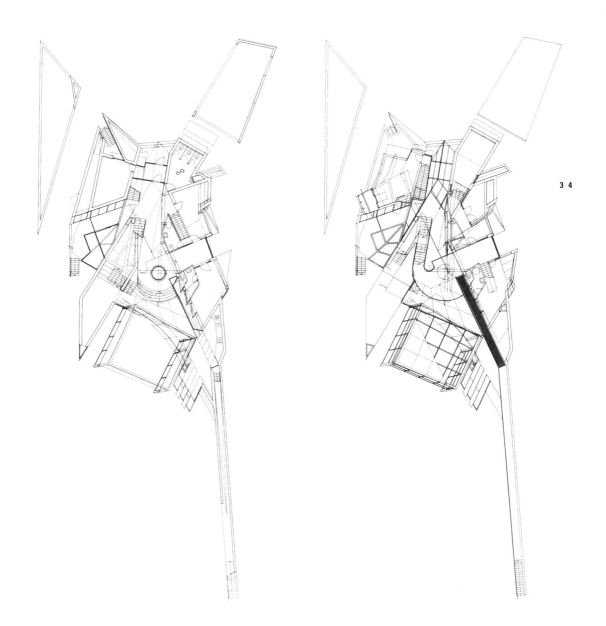

3 4

3. Ground floor plan
4. First floor plan
5. Interior [photo: G.v.B.]
6. Axonometric of the main mass of the building

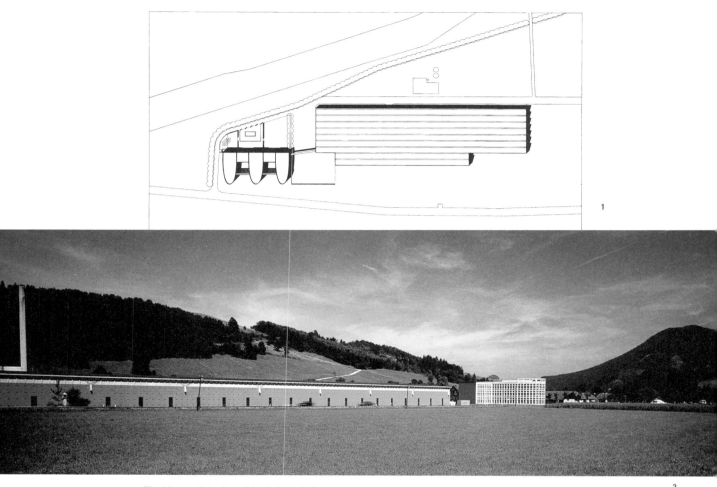

1

2

The idea and design of both the administrative and factory building commissioned by the internationally renowned company Bene Büromöbel are founded on a basic reflection on the place of everyday work, on office life. They illustrate this rare corporate culture that embodies corporate identity from the product to the building as an "experiment on one's own body". Ortner Bene's buildings – as well as the showrooms in Vienna – represent basic statements, in which the production of cultural significance accompanied by professional anonymity formulate the objective. Through their intelligent application and combination, robust and simple tectonic elements create an emotional and metaphorical atmosphere. The concrete prefabs, which make up the facade and the semi-elliptical shape of the structure, obscure the scale, the building complex leads an archaic fundamental dialogue with its surroundings.

Bene Administration and Factory

Ortner & Ortner
Waidhofen, Lower Austria, 1986-88

1. Site plan
2. Factory
3. Administration building
[photos: J.P.]

An old shed on the premises of the Austrian Research Centre Seibersdorf was to be turned into an office building and reflect the work of an interdisciplinary expert group. Simultaneity lies in the work systems and architecture. The tectonic elements were mixed, not just randomly, but "simultaneously". With various supports, volumes, skins, spaces in-between. The extension of the room toward the outside is also physically experienced by the observer. The sheath of the beam, which gives shape to the room, is pulled over the thermal and sound insulation shells, reaching all the way to the outer skin made of layered trapezoidal sheet metal. Zinked grid elements enfold the building structure as an inner and outer sheath.

Office Building
Coop Himmelb(l)au
Seibersdorf, Lower Austria, 1993–95

1. From the north-east
2. From the north-west
[photos: G.Z.]

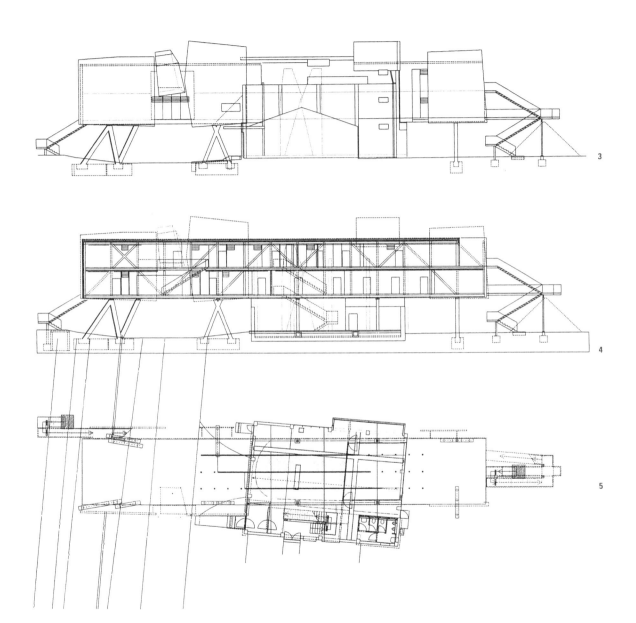

3. Ground floor plan
4. Longitudinal section
5. Northwest elevation
6. From the southwest [photo: G.Z.]

In small-scale airports ritualized activities can be carried out at a distance while keeping the object within range of sight. This concept of spatial arrangement is based on the parameters of the range of sight. For a start, it was necessary to build a continuous shed-type roof with a skylight and clearly distinguishable built-in units that guarantee a clear view. Since the project involved the extension of an existing complex, a wide aisle was cut into the existing stock to guarantee a clear view of the entire range. In contrast to the customary procedure with airports, the application of an altogether drafted world and the removal of any spatial references was avoided. One could also say that in this case architecture recaptures lost territory: space as sensual experience.

1

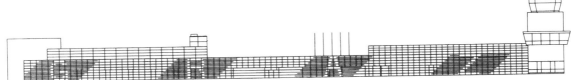

2

Graz Airport
Florian Riegler
Roger Riewe
Graz, Styria, 1992–94

1. East elevation, entrance side
2. West elevation, airfield side
3. Facade towards the airfield [photo: P.O.]
pp. 166-167:
4. Facade towards the driveway [photo: P.O.]
5. Sections

4

5

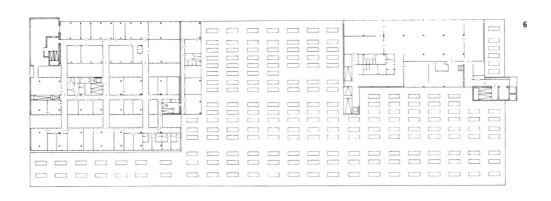

6

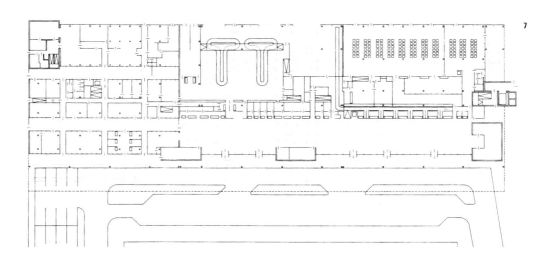

7

6. Upper level plan
7. Ground floor plan
8. Departure hall [photo: P.O.]

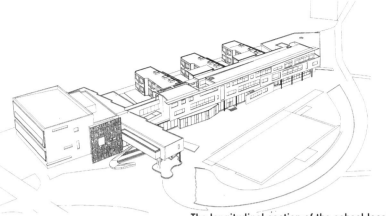

1

The longitudinal section of the school located south of Vienna, near the southeastern ring road, closes off a plot of open land bounded by large, tall trees. In front lie the playground, a sports field and a pond. The school structure is suggestive of a comb. The orderly arrangement is overtoned by numerous, intentionally introduced swings, slants, misalignments, proturbances and contractions. They furnish the primary structure with a differentiated spatial pattern. A stroll through the building reveals colours (advised by Oskar Putz) that now and again shift the accent from the exterior to the interior. Modern educational requirements are met in the group rooms and the highly differentiated corridor zone provides much open space. The school's posture exhibits playfulness and pluralism.

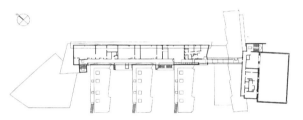

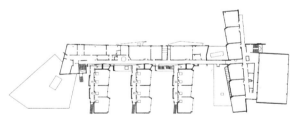

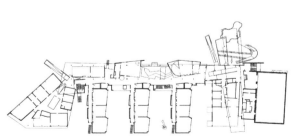

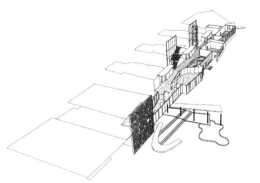

2 3

Absberggasse
Basic Secondary School
Rüdiger Lainer
Vienna, 1992-94

1. Perspective from the southwest
2. Second, first and ground floor plans
3. Sequence of rooms at the ground floor
4. Main entrance, with gymnasium [photo: M.S.]

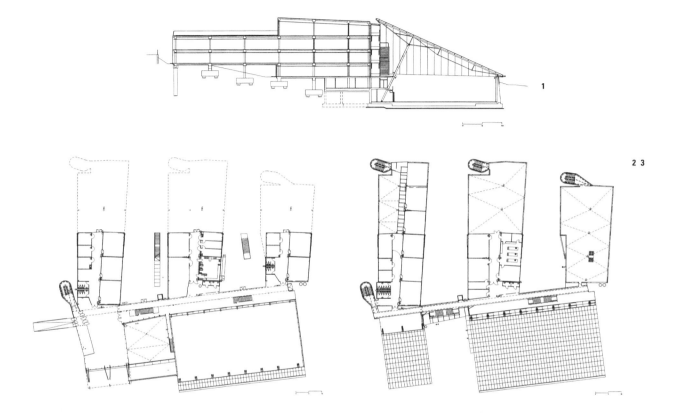

"I wanted to build a school that does not reveal the uncomfortable element
so characteristic of schools at first glance." (Helmut Richter)
From afar, the two wedge-shaped glass elements that enfold the entrance hall
and gym are plainly and clearly visible. The steel construction, spanning a
distance of 18 metres, has been minimized to an extreme, producing a filigree
and airy structure. The classroom sections are designed as concrete skeletons
with prefab ceilings, while industrial steel elements and aluminum sliding
windows were used for the facades. The classrooms were arranged in the
conventional manner, to give undisturbed classes, while the remaining area
is clearly laid out and transparent.

Kink-Platz
Basic Secondary School
Helmut Richter
Vienna, 1992–95

1. Section through north-south
2. Ground floor plan
3. Third floor plan
4. Gymnasium [photo: M.E.]
5. From the south [photo: M.E.] pp. 174-175

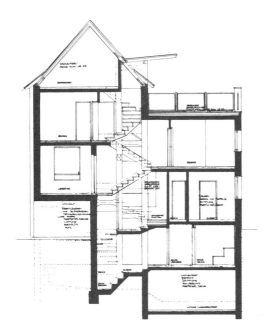

A single family home in the Vienna suburbs which looks like its surrounding houses – complete with saddle-back roof, canopy, small building extensions, light-coloured roughcast, seemingly carelessly positioned windows – is actually no model to show off with, if it were not for the highly skilled combination of intensely interwoven spatial arrangement with a sublimely controlled building structure. The design rules and their implementation constitute the mannerism inherent to the house, which however, is only the design background for the actual confrontation of the building and living: "Architecture is not life. Architecture is backdrop. Anything else is not architecture." (Hermann Czech)

M. House
Hermann Czech
Schwechat, Lower Austria, 1977-81

1. Section
2. Ground floor
3. From the east
[photos: A.C.]

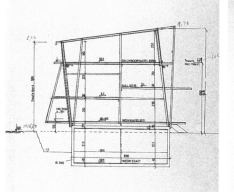 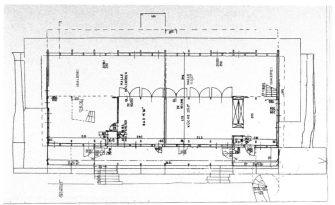

The scenery in Moos, which lies in the province of Salzburg, is no longer unspoiled: a high-voltage line crosses the valley on huge pylons one hundred metres east of the construction grounds; the highway passes three hundred metres to the west. The simple structure of the blueprint is perceived best in the sectional drawing. Eleven wooden frames define one large room. Several side rooms are separated from it. Basically, it is a kind of loft that allows subdivisions at a later time. The construction imitates the carpentry of farm buildings.

The design takes the frame of a modern barn and modifies it to become a residential building. A process of construction results that takes into account both the costs and benefits of the simplest possibilities. This intelligent assembly of random material is architecture.

Duplex House Glanegg
Max Rieder
Groedig, Salzburg, 1990–92

1. Upper level interior
2. Section
3. Ground floor plan
4. From the east
[photos: M.S.]

The existing set of classrooms was extended and a new section with workshops and more classrooms was added to the Vocational Commercial College in Bregenz. The complex is U-shaped and has a low two-storeyed intermediate block with café and a multipurpose hall connecting the old school with the new building. The workshops were accommodated in a five-storey building measuring 128 m long and enveloped in a sheath of pure glass. On the side of the railway tracks, the glass sheath is glazed with a fine horizontal trellis made of aluminum lamellae, while the courtside wears a two-shelled facade with an outer scaled armour made of glass. The extension of the old school building proudly presents its green Eternit facade.

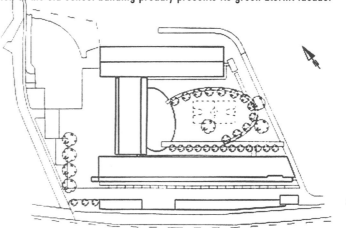

2

Provincial Vocational College
Dietmar Eberle
Karl Baumschlager
Bregenz, Vorarlberg, 1993-94

1. From the railway side
2. Site plan
3. Courtyard side
[photos: E.H.]

4

This is the third energy-related building by Bétrix-Consolascio in Salzburg after the first thermal power station and the substation. The building presents itself as a cast form, a concentration of volume disseminating an atmosphere of gravity. The intention was to find out how concrete and stainless steel can interact. The steel plates stand next to each other without overlapping and are welded together on all sides. These somewhat irregular lines correspond to the partially washed-out seams between the form-work elements of the concrete walls. The building's position is determined by the location of the railway tracks. Even the raised and newly faced chimney is oriented along their lines. A surprising element is the distorted front view of a building which otherwise has an orthogonal outline in the ground plan.

Power Station
Marie-Claude Bétrix, Eraldo Consolascio, Eric Maier with Guido Züger
Salzburg, 1992-95

1. North elevation
2. East elevation
3. Longitudinal section
4. From the south [photo: E.H.]
5. From the south-east [photo: D.C.]

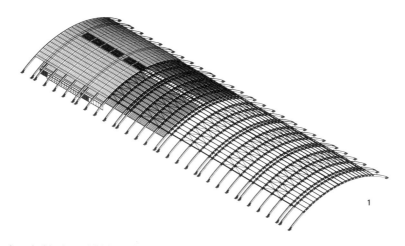

1

The Centre is suitable for exhibitions, fairs, conferences, and festive events of all kinds. From the outside it appears only as a glass roof. Arches of steel span clear over an area measuring the size of two soccer pitches. The glass roof is an intelligent tectonic sheath. Together with the light engineer Christian Bartenbach, Herzog+ Partner developed a glass insulating system with a retroreflecting grid that deflects the sun's direct rays while remaining permeable to the sky's diffuse light. The seemingly weightless girder construction gives the visitor the impression of moving in a diffuse penumbra, shielded from the climate and weather. The organization of the ground plan is rational and straightforward. Fields of space that can be used for various purposes are marked out.

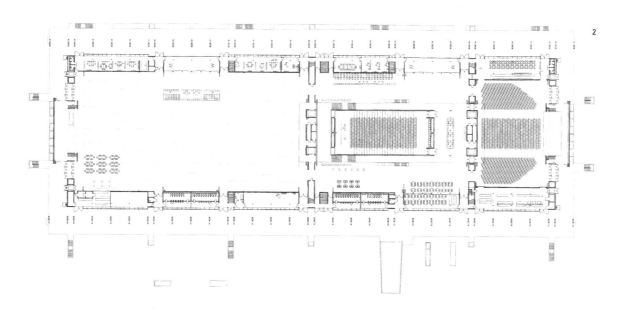

2

Design Centre

Thomas Herzog
Linz, Upper Austria, 1988, 1991-93

1. Roof, construction diagram
2. Ground floor plan
3. Aerial view [photo: D.L.]

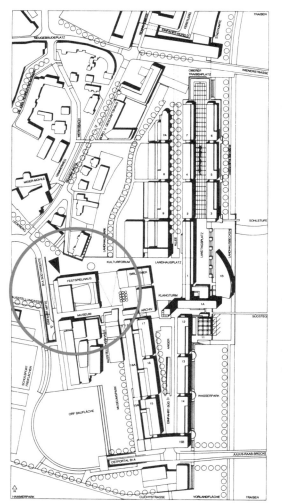

The new Festspielhaus (Auditorium) constitutes the pivot of a new cultural district that links the government quarter, which was built at the banks of the Traisen river in only five years, with the old baroque and fin-de-siècle parts of this up-and-coming medium-sized town. It is primarily a concert hall but also functions as an opera, musical theatre, ballet and theatre. Kada's vision was to create an "open house", to peel the main performance hall from the building mass, thus revealing an "iridescent crystal", to show it symbolically and at the same time make the building mass appear light. "I also associated the project with a brightly lit circus tent, which towers over the main square, while the service wagons, the service areas dock around it".

The enormous mass of the doubly curved concrete shell thus appears astoundingly light and floating because it is enveloped in a backlighted skin of enamel glass.

Auditorium
Klaus Kada
St Pölten, Lower Austria, 1992-97

1. Site plan
2. From the north-east [photo: A.K.]

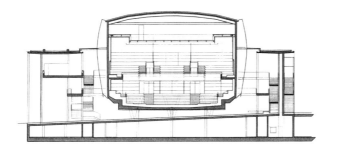

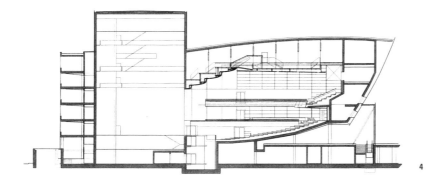

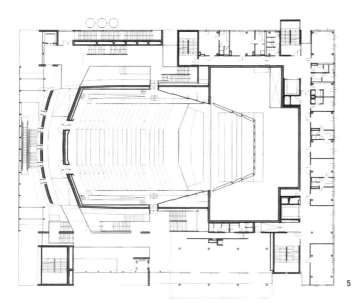

3. Cross section
4. Longitudinal section
5. Second level plan
6. From the east [photo: R.S.]
7. Grand auditorium [photo: A.K.]

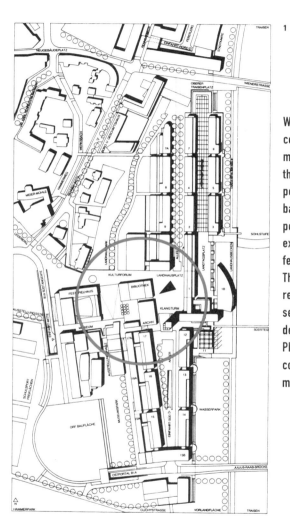

With the envelope of an extremely strict and introverted composition of buildings, the architects used simple means to create powerful and convincing ambiances in the different rooms: the main library hall is a contemporary pendant to the splendid libraries of the province's baroque cloister with its sophisticated skylight positioning, the generous north window to the city, the excellent blend of study room, club atmosphere, and the festive magnificence of sites dedicated to public culture. The ascetic calm and abundance of light in the archive's reading room and staircase also hint at enlightened, secularized monasticism. As a whole and with the dexterously integrated allusions to Scarpa, Siza and Plecnik, these buildings constitute an essential contribution within the scope of the trans-modern, minimalist architecture of contemporary Austria.

Federal Library & Archives of Lower Austria

Karin Bily
Paul Katzberger
Michael Loudon
St Pölten, Lower Austria, 1992-97

1. Site plan
2-3. From the west and east: library and archive [photo: R.S.]

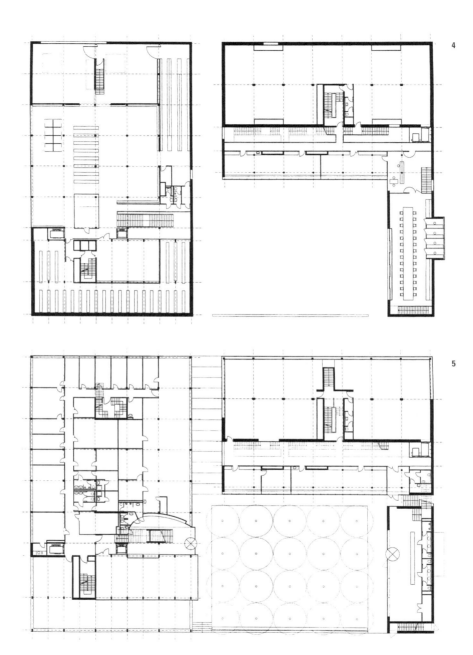

4. First floor plan, reading level, library & archive
5. Ground floor plan, library & archive
6. Archive, reading room
7. Stairway towards archive
[photos: R.S.]

ARTEC's central theoretical themes – "the search for simple basic elements; an appreciation of the right angle; the full-format employment of materials, turning disadvantages to advantages" – are minimalist and at the same time able to react clearly and powerfully to existing rooms and structures. Their school building in Vienna fills the site to its margins and divides asymmetrically into two contrasting typologies according to the surrounding stipulations that remain linked through the spinal cord of the multi-storey access hall in which room heights, outlooks, and lights channels pulsate in all directions.

The autonomy of the "brutal" construction and material language stands dialectically to the subtle, non-narrative, primarily functional interpretation of the site.

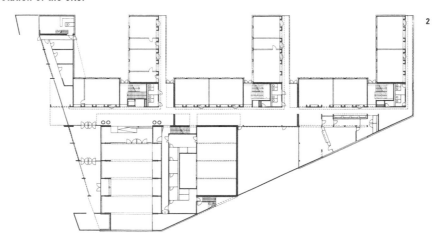

Zehdengasse Elementary School
ARTEC [Bettina Götz, Richard Manahl]
Vienna, 1995–96

1. Aisle
2. Ground floor plan
3. From the west, entire building area
4. From the south
[photos: R.S.]

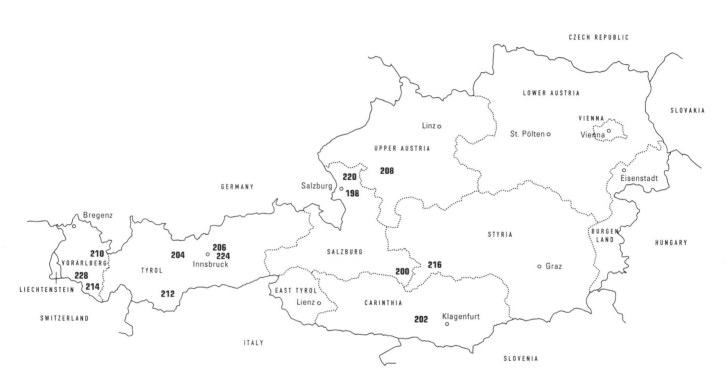

CZECH REPUBLIC

LOWER AUSTRIA

SLOVAKIA

Linz ○

St. Pölten ○

VIENNA

Vienna ○

UPPER AUSTRIA

220

Salzburg ○ **198**

208

Eisenstadt ○

GERMANY

STYRIA

BURGEN LAND

HUNGARY

Bregenz ○

210

206

224

Innsbruck ○

SALZBURG

216

200

Graz ○

VORARLBERG

204

TYROL

228

214

212

EAST TYROL

Lienz ○

CARINTHIA

LIECHTENSTEIN

202

Klagenfurt ○

SWITZERLAND

ITALY

SLOVENIA

Austria is a holiday destination because it still has a largely intact, beautiful and diverse landscape. The tourist industry is one of the most important economic factors for the country. Architects interpret this landscape and specific locations within it and in so doing, they come into conflict with today's clichés about tourism as well as the formalism of the countryside and town statutes created for it. Creative dialogue with the landscape was and is one of the special challenges of Austrian architecture. Lois Welzenbacher's country house and Ernst Plischke's house on Atter Lake completely redefine the elementary qualities of landscape-oriented building. On the other hand, Clemens Holzmeister adopts and reinterprets the romantic air of traditional forms of building. These modern examples arise from both main roots of the time between the wars and use up-to-date materials.

The one source with the most artistic power is true understanding and use of nature.
Understanding each building in the spirit of the landscape, (the balance between the building and its surroundings can be made conspicuous with simple, yet effective mathematical methods) results in diverse and ever-changing architectural design.
LOIS WELZENBACHER

The beauty of nature and the way we respond to it today is in a way a luxury arising from the final phase of our absolute domination of the environment. Environmental protection, i.e. nature's dependence on human kind for protection, is an indication of this. It is therefore questionable whether we should really use the term "natural" for the landscape, as it is the product of thousands of years of processing by humans.
FRIEDRICH ACHLEITNER

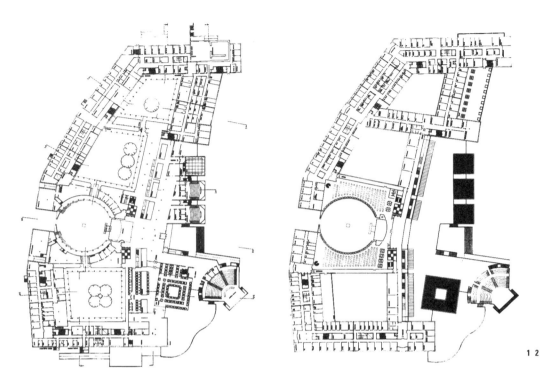

1 2

The principle of wing architecture, quite practicable for the given task of moving a faculty of natural science
of the University of Salzburg to a new residence, is translated into a series of public building elements
and applied to define the relationship with the joint central areas. The arrangement of rooms, starting from
the forecourt, leads over the monumental, cylindrical entrance yard to the glass hall and splays out, rising
with projecting staircases to the galleries of the individual storey, at the front of which south-facing
greenhouses filter the sunlight, flowing into the panorama landscape with the terraces and the auditorium
blocks. In allusion to the theatrical sequence of space in Salzburg's old city, Holzbauer successfully
compiles royal and bourgeois scenarios, urban typology, and stylized parkscape into a mannerist collage.

Faculty of Natural Sciences
Wilhelm Holzbauer
Salzburg, 1982–86

1. Ground floor plan
2. Second floor plan
3. From the north, general view [photo: M.P.-D.]

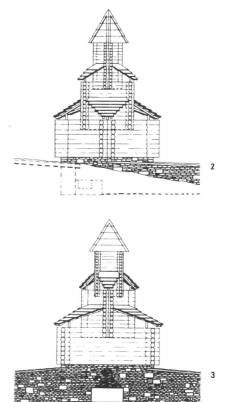

The environment, reason, idea, material, and actual construction of this mountain chapel for foresters determine each other. The structure is defined by the triangular floor plan, into which Maria Bilger has incorporated her images of a tripolar world. However, the chapel is more: the foresters' "archaic world", a reference to the countryside churches with painted wooden ceilings, the visionary geometry that has always stimulated the building trade and fed spatial fantasy, filtered by memories from the stave churches to the wooden Slovak churches, of the stacked cupolas characteristic of Moldavian monasteries to Guarini's spatial visions, of Plecnik to Perret, and the diversity of Islamic construction. In spite of the flood of memories, this is a new idea being presented, developed from the historical memory of Central Europe.

1. Ceiling painting by Maria Bilger-Kurrent
2. Side elevation
3. Front elevation
4. Side view
[photos: F.W.]

Mountain Chapel
Friedrich Kurrent
Ramingstein, Salzburg, 1990–91

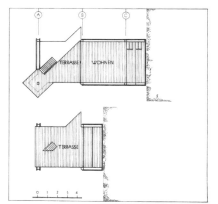

1 2

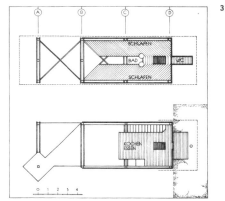

3

As soon as one catches sight of the house on the steep hillside over the Ossiacher Lake, one invariably compares it to the old barns and farms located in the immediate surroundings and enjoying a similar topographical situation. Self-assured, they display themselves facing the valley, offering as small a target as possible to the slope - just as the new house Manfred Kovatsch built for the artist Cornelius Kolig. A wooden construction planked with larch wood on three sides. The house opens exclusively toward the valley and the grand Alpine panorama through a filter of terraces, open staircases and seats. It celebrates the feeling of a home in a place that sways continuously between safety and danger and does not trivialize the situation of being exposed.

1. From the northwest, looking at Ossiacher Lake [photo: F.A.]
2. Level 3 + 4 plans
3. Level 1 + 2 plans
4. From the southeast [photo: A.Ko.]

Kolig House
Manfred Kovatsch
Ossiacher Lake, Carinthia, 1975-77

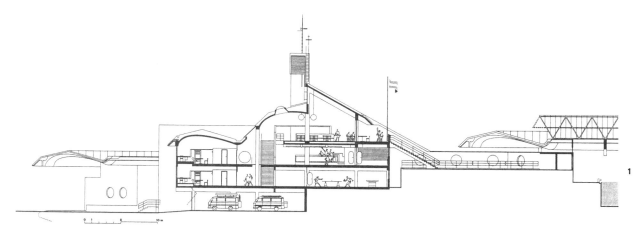

The convent's two towers are the most prominent features of the small Tyrolian town of Stams. The ski gymnasium stands at a right angle to the convent and parallel to the slope, underscoring the topographically determining edge. The white wall, whose levelness is emphasized by round apertures, is completed by the band of windows as a shady zone of the roof. Two elegantly swung concrete shells are separated by a glazed skylight. Underneath lies an internal street, which accesses almost all rooms. The building structure also displays symbolism which is comprehensible by association. The floor plan of the building is suggestive of a bishop's staff and the cross section of the roof is reminiscent of an eagle's spread wings. Austria's elite ski jumpers and skiers are trained in the Stams skiing gymnasium.

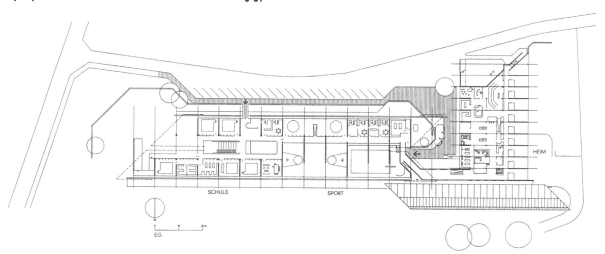

Sports Gymnasium
Othmar Barth
Stams, Tyrol, 1977–82

1. Section through dormitory wing
2. Ground floor plan
3. School yard [photo: A.B.]

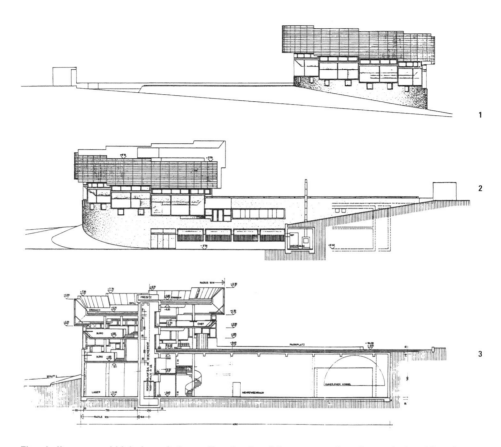

1

2

3

The challenge: a rubbish dump between the street and the construction site, an isolated location in the central mountain ridge of northern Tyrol, and the complex construction programme. The object consists of one large spirally designed office spanning four floors with an elevator shaft in the centre and an accompanying spiral staircase. The building is accessed at medium height from a square at the front. The large, cylindrical room is presented with various lighting conditions and vistas by the slightly misaligned sectors and the smooth directional transition, which necessitate a variety of lighting installations. This office building is an ideal form of construction, resulting from the relationship between function and environment successfully set into the natural landscape.

Bartenbach Light Studio
Josef Lackner
Aldrans, Tyrol, 1986–88

1. North elevation
2. South elevation
3. Section
4. From the south [photo: C.L.]

The idea and the entire concept of the facility has its origins in the classical lakeside and bath house architecture of the Salzkammergut where the provinces of Salzburg, Upper Austria, and Styria meet - an area abundant in lakes. The arch-like row of cabins at the banks of the lake creates a bathing and sunning court with a protective element at the northern end. At the western end of the arch lies a two-storeyed, semicircular construction element with sanitary facilities, a roofed open area at ground level, and a sauna whose roof serves as a sun terrace. At the eastern limits of the complex lies a bath house. In the "protected" proliferation of formal elements falsely interpreted as touristy and regionalistic, special attention is paid to modest and cultivated solutions. They are, after all, reminiscent of a time when the "guest" was still met with deference.

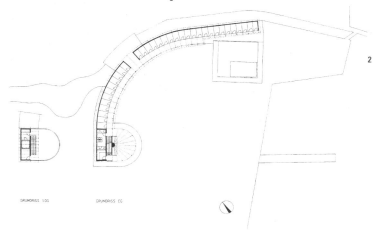

Lakeside Facility Häupl
Maximilian Luger
Franz Maul
Attersee Lake, Upper Austria, 1990-91

1. Changing rooms wing
2. Upper level plan, ground floor plan
3. Entire building complex
[photos: K.K.]

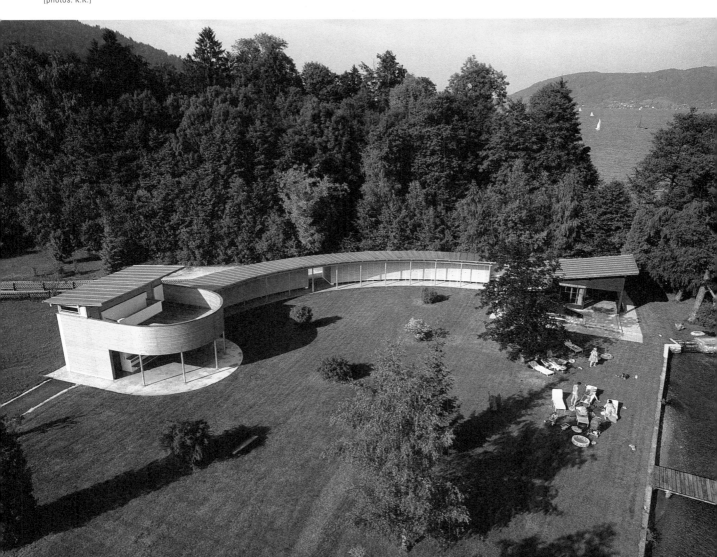

1

Warth is a village of mountain farmers at an altitude of 1500 m on the Arlberg, which has advanced to become a fashionable ski resort. The new school holds only two classes, but also all the required special rooms. The building is located at the edge of a slope and on the only (and therefore prized) plateau of the community area. To preserve level ground for games, sports and festivals, and also to enlarge this area, the new building was set onto the adjacent slope, its functions were stacked vertically into a compact volume. The resulting architecture is tailored to meet prevailing conditions and its holistic approach takes care to include every little detail including to the newly developed furnishings. The building appears conventional, but all in all it has much more to show than everyday architecture. A key contribution to the architectural scene of Vorarlberg.

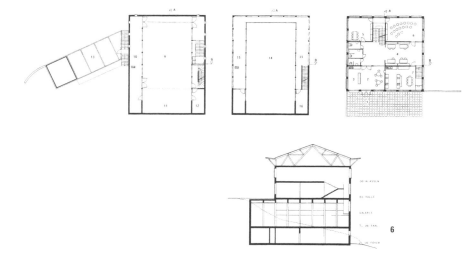

2 3 4 5

6

Primary and Basic Secondary School
Roland Gnaiger
Warth, Vorarlberg, 1991–92

1. From the northeast
2. First underground level
3. Gallery level plan
4. Ground floor plan
5. Upper level plan
6. Section
7. From the east
[photos: M.S.]

The architect's work involved both a construction concept for a new part of Mandarfen and the plans for the hotels. Two conditions were decisive: numerous avalanche tracks restrict the availability of narrow tracks of land, and a chairlift traverses the construction site. The building concept provided for seven family hotels and a small centre. The proposal was accompanied by a design catalogue defining roof shape and cladding, entrances, open staircases, materials, and colours of the outer walls. The two hotels built by the architects bear witness to Austria's new proud stance in tourism.

1. Hotel Vier Jahreszeiten
2. Hotel Vier Jahreszeiten, second floor plan
3. Alpinhotel, first floor plan
4. Alpinhotel
[photos: S.S.]

Hotel Vier Jahreszeiten and Alpinhotel
Alois and Elena Neururer
Mandarfen, Tyrol, 1991-92

The base, which also serves as mountain cabin and hotel, lies at an altitude of 2040 metres above the Silvretta reservoir (Bielerhöle, Vorarlberg) and refers to the existing topography and dam wall. The swing of the house's front facade follows the contour lines and opens its rooms to the view in a fan-like manner. The straight back wall is made of protective reinforced concrete. Generous cascade-like stairs link the different storeys. The roof is suggestive of hotels built in the 1930s, but, the panel with sun collectors bring us back to modern times. The designers attempted to link up, where they assume autonomous building in the Alps still exists - before the touristic Fall of Man.

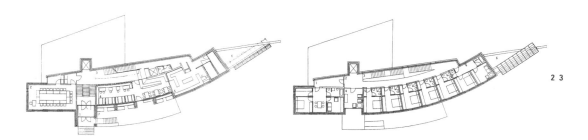

1. From the northeast
2. Ground floor plan
3. Second floor plan
4. From the south
[photos: A.Be.]

Silvretta House
Much Untertrifaller jr.
Gerhard Hörburger
Bielerhöhe, 1991–92

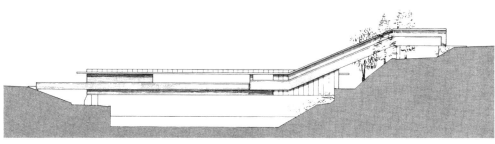

The exhibition concept of the Styrian Provincial Exhibition 1995 "Holzzeit" (Timber Time) included plans to erect a new wooden bridge spanning 47 metres. The design provided for a primary support framework, protected against weathering and intended to have a long service life. It was to be equipped with lateral shear walls and secondary elements for the roadway and the guard rail which, if damaged, could be replaced after several decades. From the urban point of view, the building closes the river in the central area. With its strong spatial character the pathway relates to the two sides of the river which are of different heights. From both river banks, two ramps access the bridge, they meet at the large "window space" over the river where the most impressive view of the city and Murau castle can be enjoyed.

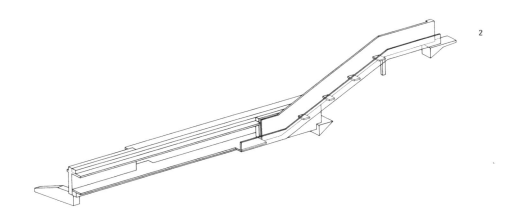

Footbridge over the Mur
Marcel Meili
Markus Peter
Jürg Conzett
Murau, Styria, 1993-95

1. Axonometric of the load-bearing structure
2. Elevation towards the city
3. General view overlooking the city [photo: M.S.]

4. Detail
5. From the north bank
[photos: M.S.]

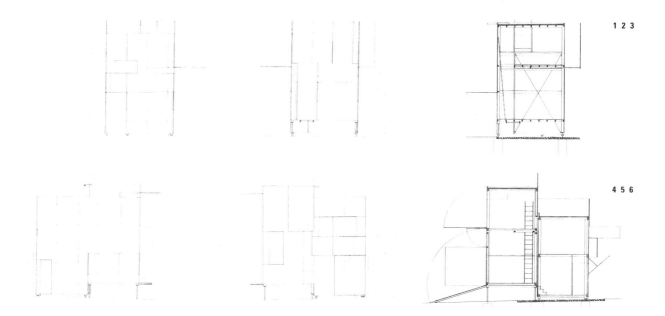

1 2 3

4 5 6

The name of the building stems from the neighboring Guglhupf mountain. The building, a walkable sculpture in deliberation with architecture and art, was erected on private property near the Mondsee Lake on the occasion of the "Festival of Regions" in 1993. The edifice, a wooden beam-and-lintel construction with plywood panelling has no windows, doors or steep roof when closed off and when seen from the lake is reminiscent of a wooden box, placed in the middle of the landscape. But this house, bath house or sculpture changes continuously when the wooden panels are opened. They can be turned, drawn, folded, and tipped in all directions: ramps, doors, windows, terraces and hatchways emerge. The atmosphere within the sculpture changes depending on the state of the openings: nature flows into and through the room, mirror images and shadows are created, and a new perception of nature is provided through all the new vistas. Public pressure caused the building to be removed.

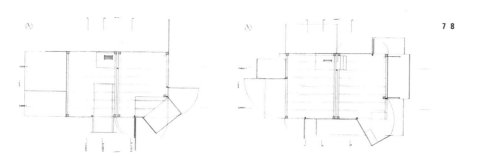

7 8

1. South elevation
2. North elevation
3. Cross section
4. East elevation
5. West elevation
6. Longitudinal section
7. 1/2 level plan
8. 3/4 level plan
9. Metamorphosis
10. Open position p. 222
11. Closed position p. 223
[photos: P.O.]

GucklHupf
Hans-Peter Wörndl
Lake Mondsee, Salzburg, 1993

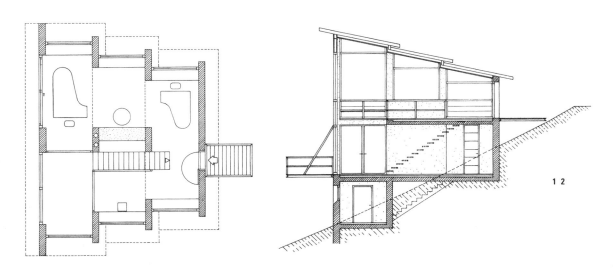

1 2

The house, made of crude concrete which submits to the inclination of the steep slope, is characterized by three layers, arranged one behind the other on the slope. The house is intended for a musician and composer and opens like a funnel to all sides of the valley.

The concrete structure is virtually persuaded to lightness by the large glazed element with slim wooden frames that give a lateral view of the valley landscape. The house interior is characterized by the prominent position of a grand piano in the gallery, where not only the magnificent view of the surrounding country can be enjoyed but the reference to the lower floor is also given. A small projecting terrace, accessible from the lower floor, further emphasizes the opening and proximity to the expanse of the surrounding mountains.

Studio for a Musician and Composer
Margarethe Heubacher-Sentobe
Weerberg-Innerst, Tyrol, 1995-96

1. Upper level plan
2. Cross section
3. From the east
4. Looking from the upper level to the lower level p. 226
5. Fog view p. 227
[photos: M.S.]

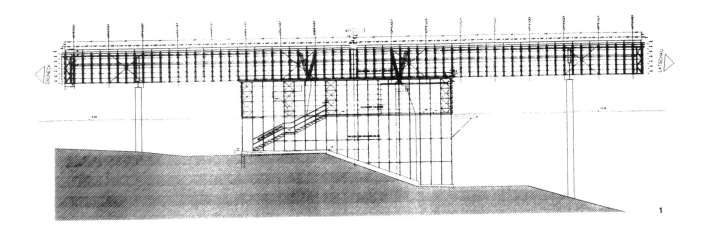

1

In view of a growing tourism industry and increased awareness of environmental matters, technical facilities in high mountain regions are faced with ever more complex requirements. For the construction of the Golmerbahn rack railway with cabins for 8 people, the existing lift line was used, old technology was reused in other places, and material use in the new construction was both economical and transparent. The mechanical, technical centre of the rack railway is enveloped by a sheath of scaled glazing with a mounting developed especially for this purpose. The facility's special feature is its coloured wooden roof construction – an idea by Karl-Heinz Ströhle. From the lively blue-red-yellow contrast of the valley station to the intermediate tones of the middle stations, this leads to the distinctly black-white station at the mountain top and provides the roof undersides with radiating lightness, producing significant kinetic colour/space effects adjusted to these altitudes that can be observed when passing by.

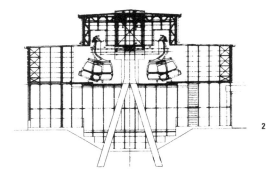

2

Golmerbahn
Leopold Kaufmann
Vandans, Vorarlberg, 1995

1. Matschwitz, southeast elevation
2. Cablecar station Grüneck, northeast elevation and main roof
3. Cablecar station Matschwitz [photo: E.H.]

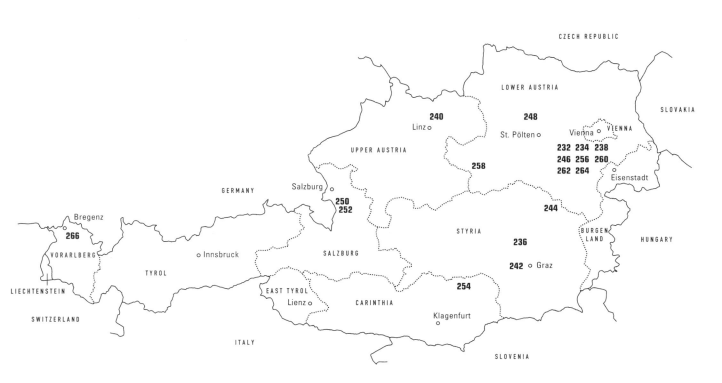

CZECH REPUBLIC

LOWER AUSTRIA

SLOVAKIA

240
Linz ○

248
St. Pölten ○

VIENNA
Vienna ○ VIENNA

UPPER AUSTRIA

232 234 238
246 256 260
262 264

258

GERMANY

Salzburg ○

250
252

Eisenstadt ○

STYRIA

244

BURGEN
LAND

Bregenz
○

266

VORARLBERG

○ Innsbruck

SALZBURG

236

HUNGARY

LIECHTENSTEIN

TYROL

242 ○ Graz

SWITZERLAND

EAST TYROL
Lienz ○

CARINTHIA

254

ITALY

Klagenfurt
○

SLOVENIA

Austria possesses a wealth of historically significant buildings. One could say that every location in this country is laden with history. Although it is not possible for official bodies to protect every historical site, since the seventies Austrians have viewed "the old" as being of far more worth than "the new." An ongoing topic of conflict in contemporary building construction in Austria is therefore the approach to the historical setting.

How should we go about developing old structures? How can newer layers be added? The examples selected here to represent of this issue illustrate contemporary responses to a sensitive and ever-present problem in the public mind.

I hate to disappoint the aesthetes: old Vienna used to be new.
KARL KRAUS

In the future, the noble edifice of tradition will continue to be enriched by the combination of a keen awareness of history and the creative ability to reformulate architectural tasks. The treatment of old structures with care and the use of foresight in constructing new buildings should result in a valuable synthesis. Our actions when building in the old part of a city should swing between respect for the historical environment and caution in the sense of foresight. If we see respect as being synonymous with the past then foresight might serve as a metaphor for the future. Somewhere between the past and the future lies the ever-changing present, the only possible basis for our actions.
FRIEDRICH KURRENT

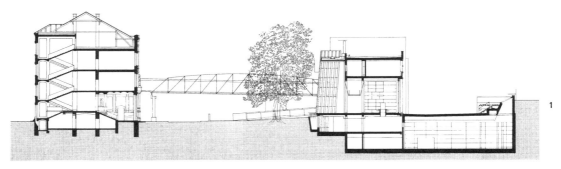

1

Behind the concrete ridges of a housing project dating back to the 1970s, a small, ordinary school building dating back to the emperor's days had survived. Now the school is faced by two new, terrace-like recessed classroom sections, linked by a articulation unit made of a large glazed hall and framed by a high, disc-like diagonal studio building. A latticed steel bridge with a glazed corridor crosses the street to the old building. The entrance to the new complex, which crosses the entry hall as a hanging bridge, is orthogonally aligned to the bridge. Podrecca's design method integrates the old building and tree stock while creating space for the autonomous new building and gaining control convincingly over a difficult urban situation.

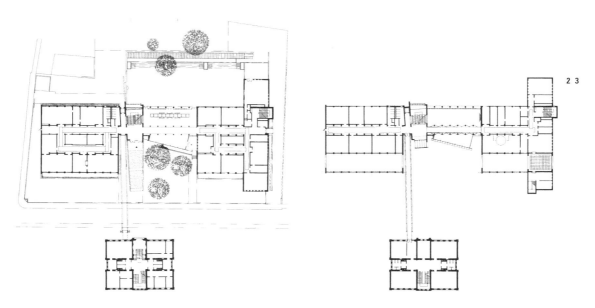

2 3

Dirmhirngasse
Basic Secondary School
Boris Podrecca
Vienna, 1992–94

1. Section
2. Ground floor plan
3. First floor plan
4. New building frontage [photo: G.Z.]

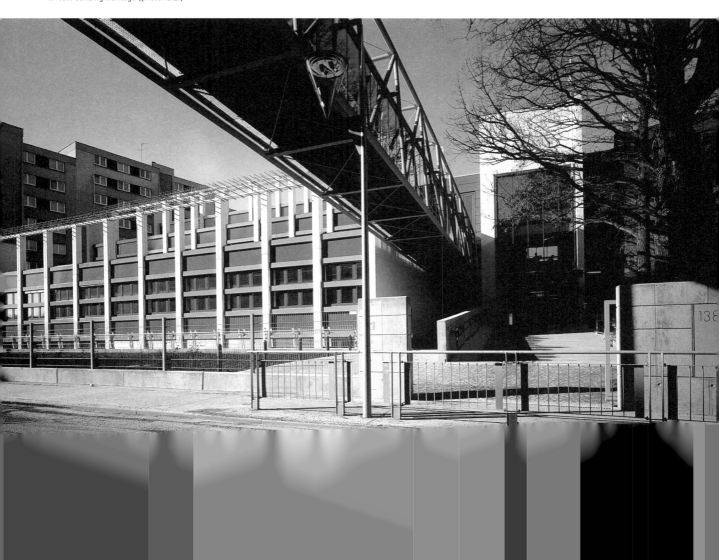

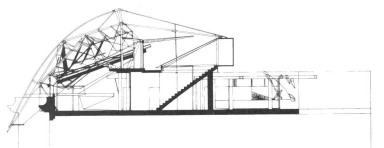

1

2

The task was to extend a lawyer's office to include the
attic and add a larger conference room and several small
offices. First there is an inspired and inspiring space,
that seems to derive its visual consistency from dynamic
forces and their resolution, and opens and introduces
vistas. The diagonal arch of the main construction
flashes through the room like lightning and is designed
like a bird's wing stretching beyond the nest. The roof
construction is also an "architecture of the site" in that
it emphasizes the effect of the airy situation above
the Ringstrasse house's eaves, and conveys not only the
experience of the house interior but also a new
experience of urban space.

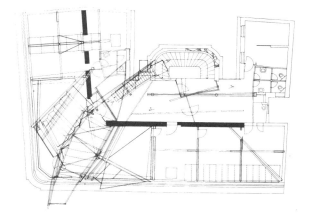

3

Roof Construction Project
Falkestrasse
Coop Himmelb(l)au
Vienna, 1983–88

1. Section
2. Location of the site
3. Plan
4. Meeting room
[photos: G.Z.]

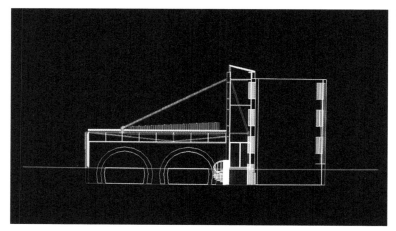

The idea was to add a laboratory hall for teaching and research to an old office building dating back to the 1950s. The building relates to its context in two ways: on the one hand by repeating the perforated front facade of the old building at the rear and having it serve as constructive element to carry the large hall roof, and on the other, through the choice of colours and materials of the steel production and their impact on the surrounding landscape. All concrete and plaster surfaces of the building exterior and interior have been coloured with slag sand. The designer sublimely translates the complex interplay of design, static, context, colour, and form into significant architecture.

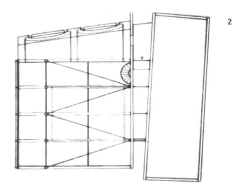

Extension Project
Laboratory Hall
Bernhard Hafner
Leoben, Styria, 1990-92

1. Cross section
2. Concept of the building and structure
3. General view [photo: B.H.]

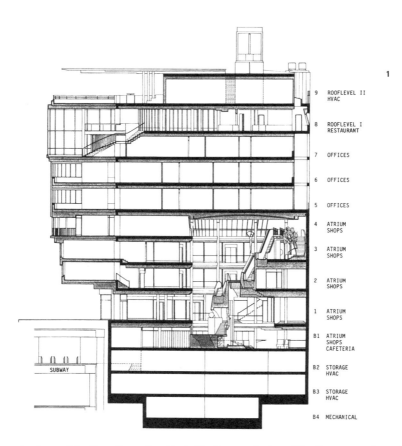

9	ROOFLEVEL II	HVAC
8	ROOFLEVEL I	RESTAURANT
7	OFFICES	
6	OFFICES	
5	OFFICES	
4	ATRIUM	SHOPS
3	ATRIUM	SHOPS
2	ATRIUM	SHOPS
1	ATRIUM	SHOPS
B1	ATRIUM	SHOPS CAFETERIA
B2	STORAGE	HVAC
B3	STORAGE	HVAC
B4	MECHANICAL	

SUBWAY

The outer form of the Haas House is adjusted to the round edge of the Roman warehouse's quadrangular, and with the bay window that accomplishes the rounded contours it forms an urban caesura between Stock-im-Eisen Square and St Stephen's Square at the heart of the city of Vienna. This was to be emphasized by columns placed out onto the square. At the same time it is an attempt to develop urbanity in the vertical by using as little space as possible. This was achieved by means of artistic finesse and high-quality materials. The artistic considerations received all sorts of impulses from innumerable legal, populist and psychological reflections. For this reason the building was also met with the reproach of being over the top. This, however, in no way disparages the pioneering role it plays for contemporary architecture, conspicuously placed at the very heart of the historical city centre.

1. Section
2. Looking towards Haas House
and St Stephans cathedral [photo: A.Ho.]

Haas House
Hans Hollein. Vienna, 1985-90

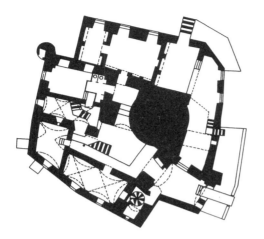 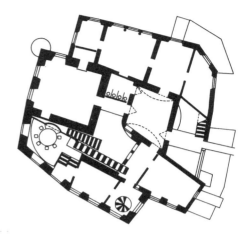

Whoever enters the Hagenberg castle (Hagenberg, Upper Austria) today is confronted by a building in which history presents itself strikingly, as a system of relationships to the contemporary age. The new quality lies in the unlocking and completion of the old room structure, in the creation of a newly organized spatial complex. This also laid the foundation for new contents, for its current use as a research institute. A kind of enlarged staircase provides a significant addition to the courtyard: new floors have been added to the baroque sheath, affording an impressive space–time experience since their dimensions correspond to those of the Middle Ages.

3

1. Ground floor plan
2. First floor plan
3. Section through west-east
4. Courtyard [photo: C.S.]

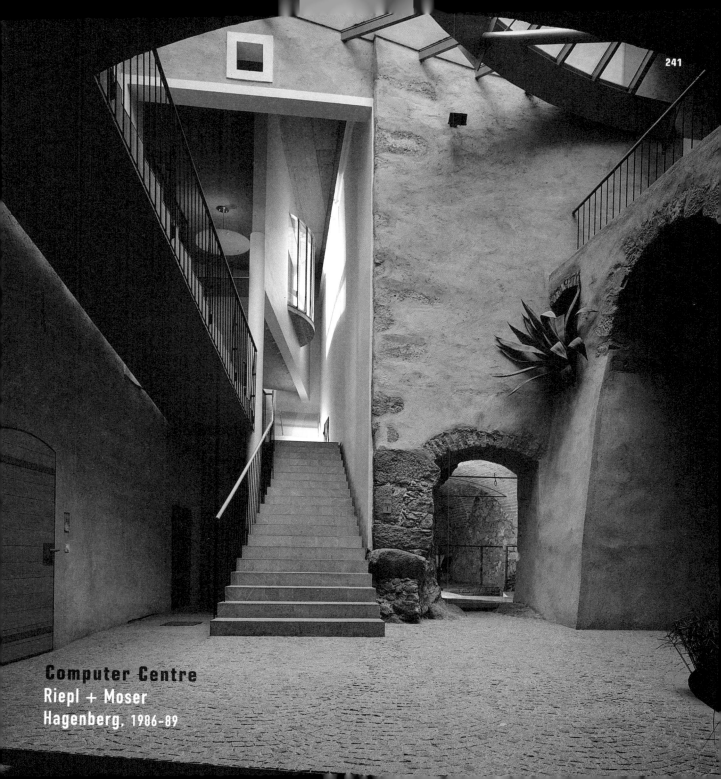

Computer Centre
Riepl + Moser
Hagenberg, 1986-89

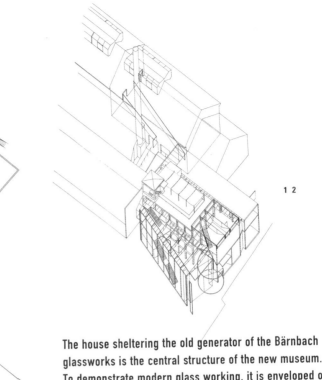

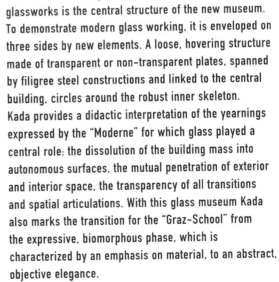

1 2

3

The house sheltering the old generator of the Bärnbach glassworks is the central structure of the new museum. To demonstrate modern glass working, it is enveloped on three sides by new elements. A loose, hovering structure made of transparent or non-transparent plates, spanned by filigree steel constructions and linked to the central building, circles around the robust inner skeleton. Kada provides a didactic interpretation of the yearnings expressed by the "Moderne" for which glass played a central role: the dissolution of the building mass into autonomous surfaces, the mutual penetration of exterior and interior space, the transparency of all transitions and spatial articulations. With this glass museum Kada also marks the transition for the "Graz-School" from the expressive, biomorphous phase, which is characterized by an emphasis on material, to an abstract, objective elegance.

Glass Museum
Klaus Kada
Baernbach, Styria, 1987–88

1. Upper level plan
2. Axonometric
3. Ground floor plan
4. From the street [photo: A.Ka.]

 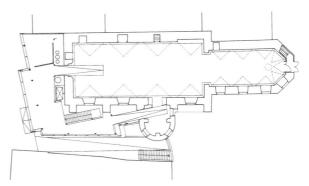

In view of its radical approach to the relationship between old and new buildings, the Kunsthaus (Arts Centre) Mürzzuschlag is unique for Austria – architecture without subjective gestures, conceived as a purely technical device. A baroque church, which was secularized 200 years ago and had almost fallen to ruin, was to be adapted on three levels for cultural events. The entrance, vestibule, administrative and side rooms are concentrated in an extension that had been added to the old building as an outer layer. This layer is suggestive of a scaffolding enveloped by a sheath of glass. Platforms, staircases and ramps keep it at a distance to the old building. Entrances, a lift, ventilation and power facilities have been succinctly placed in this interstice. The conspicuous slants of the extension resulted from purely economic considerations and complex local conditions.

Arts Centre
Konrad Frey
Mürzzuschlag, Styria, 1988-91

1. Former church, once refurbished
2. Upper level plan
3. Section through annex
4. Cross section
5. Annex
[photos: T.M.]

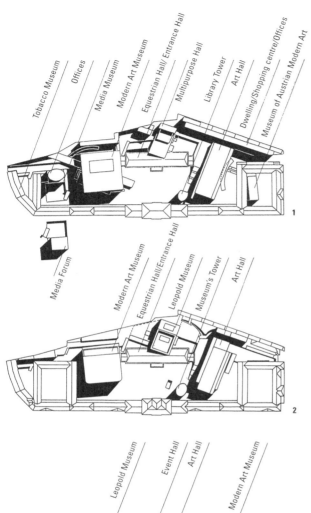

Tobacco Museum
Offices
Media Museum
Modern Art Museum
Equestrian Hall/Entrance Hall
Multipurpose Hall
Library Tower
Art Hall
Dwelling/Shopping centre/Offices
Museum of Austrian Modern Art

1

Media Forum

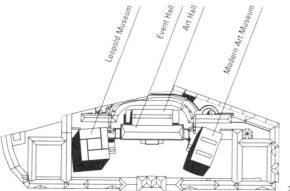

Modern Art Museum
Equestrian Hall/Entrance Hall
Leopold Museum
Museum's Tower
Art Hall

2

Leopold Museum
Event Hall
Art Hall
Modern Art Museum

3

4

In the 1980s a new attraction in urban culture was needed. This lead to the "discovery" of the deserted "imperial stables", which marks the monarchic representative centre as border of the perpetually unfinished "imperial forum". The programme for the "Museumsquartier" includes two representative museums of modern art and various other contemporary cultural interventions – art hall, event hall, media centre etc. The project by Laurids and Manfred Ortner has cleverly intertwined the urban patterns of the imperial centre with those of the neighbouring bourgeois district, a structure which enhances the value of the quarter, allows passage through and opens the site.
The Architektur Zentrum Wien was the first to establish its headquarters at this location in 1993. After many years of discussing the implementation of this project, and after several project revisions and amendments to the initial project by the architects, construction finally began in 1998.

Museumsquartier
Ortner & Ortner
Vienna, since 1990

1. Competition site, 1990
2. As of October 1994
3. As of December 1997, current state
4. Competition model, 1990 [photo: H.S.]
5. As of 1997 [photo: G.Z.]

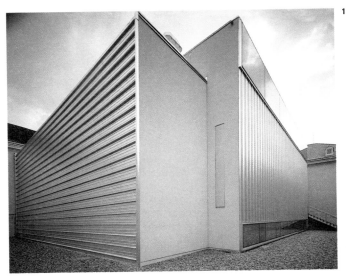

An old, angular tobacco factory building dating back to the 19th century encircles a large courtyard tangentially to the walls of the Stein prison. Two new elements, an exhibition room and a dual ramp system, envelope the glass covered courtyard and exclude the somewhat problematic neighbourhood. The new exhibition hall meets conservationist requirements that would have been impossible in the old building or would have involved high costs. The ramp system connects the two storeys of the old street section with the new yard section and the lecture hall below. The old building had already been held in high architectural esteem. The similarly laconic and precise extension stands resolutely as its equal.

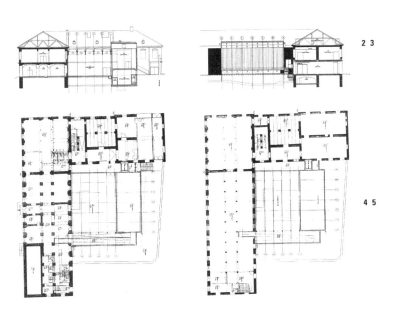

Art Centre
Adolf Krischanitz
Krems, Lower Austria, 1993–95

1. Courtyard side annex
2. Cross section through courtyard
3. Section through old building,
elevation of new exhibition wing
4. Ground floor plan
5. Upper level plan
6. Central hall with ramp beyond
[photos: M.S.]

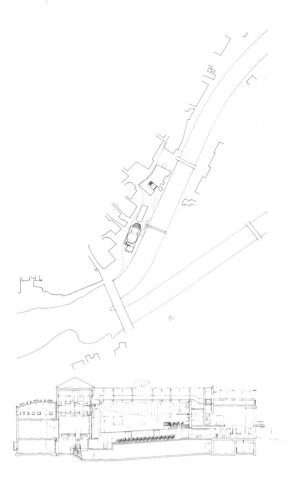

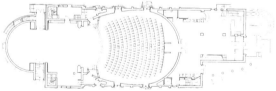

The structural alteration of the small town theatre built by Wunibald Deininger, one of Otto Wagner's students, aimed at modernizing and incorporating the building into an urban context. The foyer was enlarged to comprise two storeys, large areas were glazed, and a roof terrace was added. The spectacular new theatre hall, lined with birch, evokes the impression of being in an instrument's resonating sound box. What follows is a small cinema hall and an intimate domical area above the backstage with a starry sky consisting of small light domes and seats – designed by Heinz Tesar for this purpose.

1

2

3

1. Site plan with Celtic Museum (above) and Theatre (below)
2. Longitudinal section
3. Ground floor plan
4. From the south, showing entrance [photo: M.M.]

Town Theater & Cinema
Heinz Tesar
Hallein, Salzburg, since 1991

The Celtic Museum is accommodated in the city's oldest building, a care centre dating back to 1654. A neighbouring house and a small tower belong to the same complex. Various extension and additions have been removed and replaced by an articulated building. This joining element encompasses an airy, multistorey hall which is also entrance, lobby, viewing deck and showroom. A facade, made of exposed concrete with striking, irregularly set windows, faces the Salzach river. The hall itself presents us with a subtle play of materials involving white walls, red marble floors, staircases of exposed concrete, glazed balcony railings, and wooden handrails. The building is the first phase of a comprehensive construction concept for the Celtic Museum.

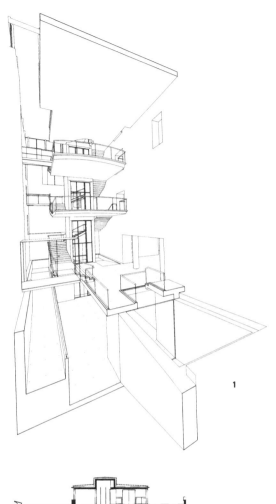

1

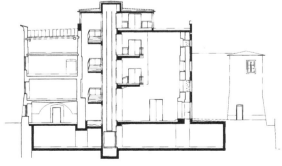

2

Celtic Museum
Heinz Tesar
Hallein, Salzburg,
since 1991

1. Perspective section
2. Cross section
3. Museum facade [photo: M.M.]

The ruins of the ironworks are a monument of the coal and steel industry. Domenig was commissioned to create an exhibition and event centre. Almost without any intervention and damage, the new functions are "suspended" between the old walls in their material simplicity and impressive form. The new is to the old the inversion of architectural means: fragile and slight to solid and heavy. Yet neither of the two disowns its industrial origin. The "suspended gallery" can be interpreted as an architectural and metaphorical symbol of the entire region. The old and new explain each other, creating a spatial adventure of almost magical nature. How much the identity of a region has been destroyed by the bombardment of mass tourism is illustrated by the intensive debate preceding the project.

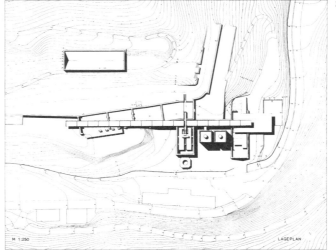

Regional Exhibition
Günther Domenig
Hüttenberg, Carinthia, 1993-95

1. Tunnel and multipurpose hall
2. Site plan
3. General view
[photos: G.Z.]

The Kleines Café, literally "small café", is a prototype for the whole lot of Vienna's architectural neuroses: as the smallest construction site Czech ever worked on, this place unites numerous chronological and intellectual layers. The inner space aptly meets expectations. Smoke traces in the vaults, worn-out stairs between the stand-up and sit-down café, reused tiles and memorial slabs worked into the floor, upholstered sofas and bentwood chairs, mirrors that are not positioned parallel to each other, dim lighting, all in an inconspicuously ingenious composition of seeming coincidences. "Architecture should not be a nuisance. The coffee house guest need not notice any of it; it could always have been that way" (Czech). This "still architecture escapes quick consumption, it is an architecture at second glance" (Dietmar Steiner).

Kleines Café
Hermann Czech
Vienna, 1970, 1973-74, 1985

1. "Kleines Café 1" (small café 1), 1970,
double mirror effects and attached ledge
2. "Kleines Café 2" (small café 2), 1974
3. Plans from 1970, 1974, 1977, 1985
[photos: A.C.]

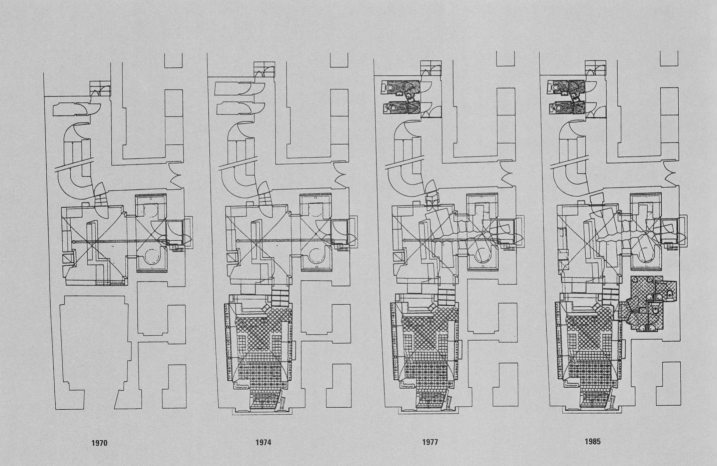

1970   1974   1977   1985

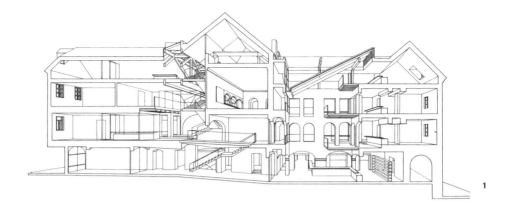

The guiding principle of the "open city hall" defined the reconstruction of the intricately grown building complex: "opening" by reducing organizational obstacles between citizens and the administration; "opening" also as a spatial, constructive intervention in an old building accessible only via stairs full of nooks and crannies. Beneder removed the vaulted ceiling above the house entrance, introduced a straight staircase, and provided the new entrance with much natural light through a glass slit in the roof. A new framework construction spans the building without intermediate supports, bears the hip roof above the main hall and the newly introduced office spaces. The new lift, wrapped in glass, rises from the vault to the framework construction, opening to a grand view of the city tower and roof landscape. The glass roofing of the courtyard arcade and its new interpretation as an open hall celebrating "civic service", perceivable from the entrance, plays an essential role.

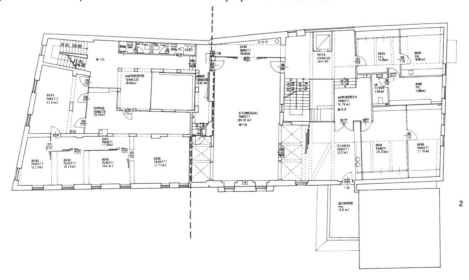

1. Sectional perspective
2. Second floor plan
3. Looking towards the city hall tower [photo: M.S.]

City Hall **(reconstruction)**
Ernst Beneder
Waidhofen/Ybbs,
Lower Austria, 1994–95

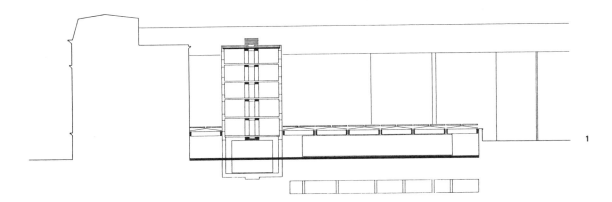

1

This private arts foundation received a new centre located in a former hat factory. The new building has been integrated into the historical backyard on the trapezoidal property. The exhibition area is located on the ground floor and is lit by daylight entering through the roof. The basement floors contain garages, storage rooms and workshops. A slanted concrete wall 30 m long divides the exhibition area and carries the roof structure. Its lamellae eliminate any direct light from the south. A plastic membrane stretching underneath acts as an additional filter and conceals the technical elements in the interstitial space. Bridge bearings cause the ceiling to be suspended four centimetres above the sharply edged concrete walls. The floor is a jointless, grey surface. The rooms and the adapted top floors for administrative purposes and studios are characterized by the reductionist scarcity of elements and their perfect elaboration to the apparent disappearance of all "details".

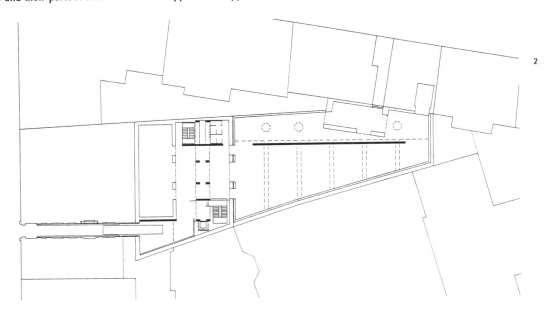

2

Generali Foundation
Christian Jabornegg
András Pálffy
Vienna, 1993-95

1. Section
2. Plan
3. Large hall [photo: W.K.]

A two-storey penthouse, as a house on top of a house, which transparently replaces the roof of the old building built in 1911, opens an unobstructed view to St Stephen's Cathedral and the Vienna Woods. Two ceiling panels – visible trapezoidal sheet metal elements with a layer of concrete in prefabricated steel frames – combine to form an open structure with numerous potential spatial configurations. The outer membrane, made of glass panels clasped between stainless steel stands, permits the interior wooden floors to pass smoothly into the outer green roofs without any thresholds. For functional reasons, the floor plan is subdivided into five sectors, allowing for various unit combinations of living and working areas. Bathrooms, kitchens and closets have been introduced as autonomous elements. A refreshing alternative to the customary roof structure as a "concrete coffin with dormer windows".

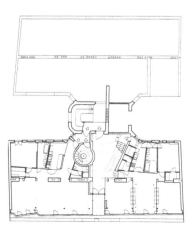
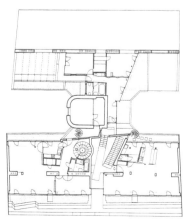

Penthouse
Rüdiger Lainer
Vienna, 1994–95

1. Night view overlooking Vienna
2. Fifth floor plan
3. Sixth floor plan
4. View from the living room
[photos: M.S.]

Through accurate interventions, the relatively tight structure of the old Palais Eskeles building was transformed into a building with ample space for exhibitions. The architects opened the yard facade and with the parabola-shaped glass shell spanning all the way up to the third floor above the former backyard created a light, multistorey indoor space – the new focus of the site. On the ground floor this internal field accommodates the lecture hall and visually includes the upper storeys. To complete this vertical element, the exhibition area on the 1st and 2nd floor was horizontally enlarged: high wall panels were placed onto the old spatial sequence casually, creating uniform identity while distributing the installation strands of the complex building technology and lighting system.

1. Sectional perspective of the courtyard
2. Exhibition space
3. Air well
[photos: M.S.]

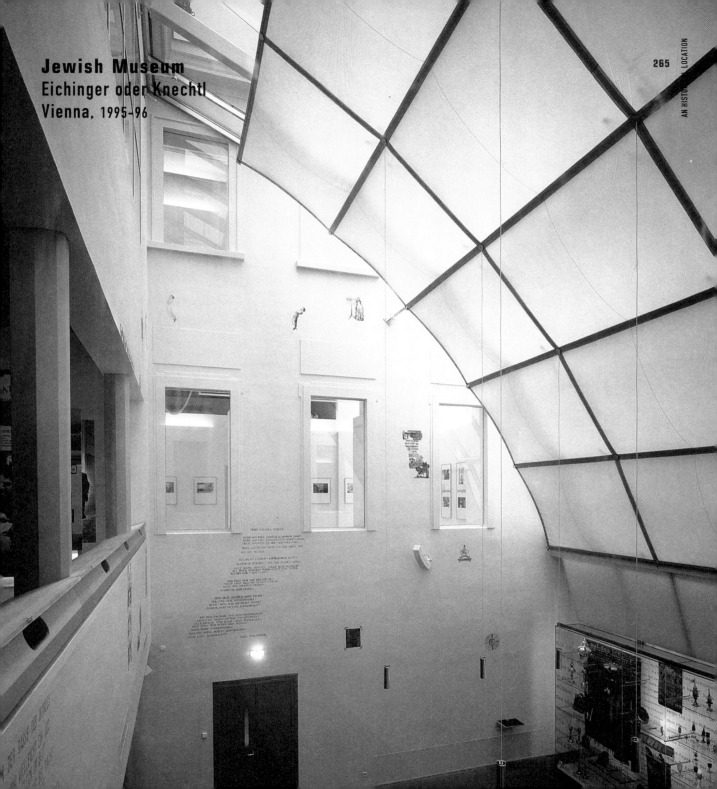

Jewish Museum
Eichinger oder Knechtl
Vienna, 1995-96

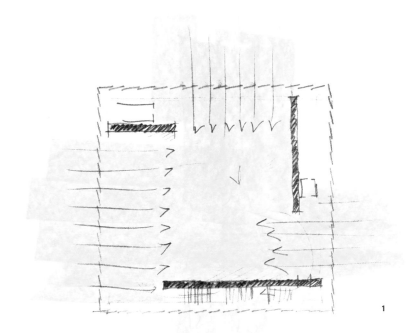

1

Facing Lake Constance, this cube enveloped in glass presents the city
with a new landmark, the low-profile service wing immediately creating
a functioning, urban focus. An uncompromising, monolithic building made
of glass, steel and concrete was built on behalf of the Vorarlberg
construction scene, a pioneer in pragmatic minimalism, as contribution
to an international competition. The specific quality of Zumthor's building
cannot be captured on photographs - and that is a compliment.
The exterior involves continuously changing mirror images of light and
atmosphere in a dialogue between building, lake and sky. The interior
involves the subtle presence of natural light in an archaically purist
but also contemporary ambiance, where no detail in the intellectual
stringency of the comprehensive concept steps out of line.
Zumthor's creed: architecture serves art best when it condenses its own
elementary values to art.

Art Centre
Peter Zumthor
Bregenz, Vorarlberg, 1994-97

1. Sketch of the incidence of light
2. Looking from lake Constance towards the Kunsthaus (Art Museum) Bregenz [photo: S.F.&H.G.]

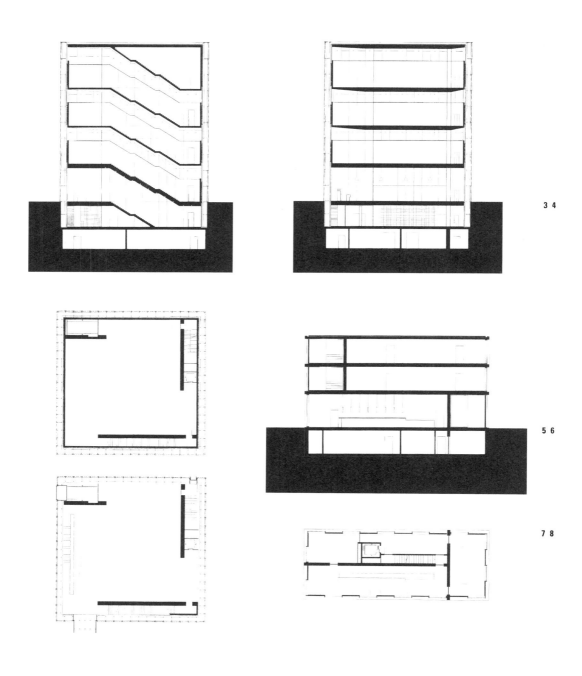

3 4

5 6

7 8

3. Section through exhibition building stairway
4. Section through exhibition building
5. Upper level exhibition space
6. Longitudinal section through administration building
7. Exhibition space, ground floor plan
8. Administration building, ground floor plan
9. Exhibition and administration building [photo: S.F.&H.G.]

10. Upper level exhibition space [photo: A.K.]
11. Looking towards the stairway of the exhibition building [photo: S.F.&H.G.]

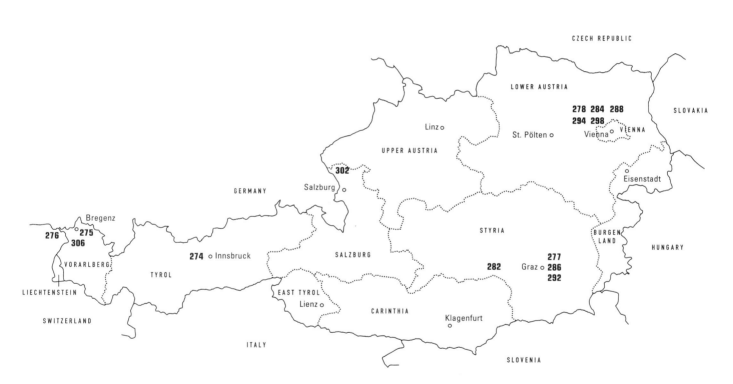

CZECH REPUBLIC

LOWER AUSTRIA

278 284 288
294 298

SLOVAKIA

Linz ○

UPPER AUSTRIA

St. Pölten ○   Vienna ○   VIENNA
                        ○ Eisenstadt

302

GERMANY

Salzburg ○

STYRIA   BURGEN-
                      LAND

Bregenz ○   HUNGARY
276 275
306   **277**
VORARLBERG   **274** ○ Innsbruck   Graz ○ **286**
                                          292
LIECHTENSTEIN   SALZBURG   **282**

SWITZERLAND   TYROL

EAST TYROL
Lienz ○

CARINTHIA
ITALY   ○ Klagenfurt

SLOVENIA

Public Housing

Austria plays a special role in residential housing. This dates back to the time between the wars, back to the "Super Blocks", the Viennese "Siedler" movement of the twenties and thirties and the disputes with the "Deutscher Werkbund." New models for contemporary residential living are particularly frequent in Vorarlberg, Styria and Vienna. Unlike in many other countries, a flat is not legally considered a commodity in Austria: it may not serve as a source of profit. Everybody is guaranteed by law the right to decent and affordable housing. However, as a consequence the free market economy tends to lose the drive for renewal in respect to improving quality and responding promptly to changing needs. The highly restrictive nature of the law inevitably leads to very high minimum standards, but it is also like a corset that tends to develop a life of its own. Since 1975, considerable effort has therefore been put into implementing modern architecture in municipal and cooperative housing as well as allowing more flexibility in codetermination, self-built homes and the realization of new ideas.

Utopian determination has little meaning and disrupts work schedules in order to go ahead with the demands of the day. Ultimately, housing reform is a political issue. The insular principles of many architects therefore seem to us to be problematic and not related to reality.
OTTO NEURATH

Innovation is possible within the constraints of publicly funded housing. The question is not one of visual utopias for a better world or even visual metaphors for an intact one; perhaps it is more about being a wolf in sheep's clothing. In order to rethink the fossilized rules in housing development and implement alternatives it is necessary to use the existing connotations of the law in such a way that they exhibit subtle variation, yet are easy for the client to agree to.
MICHAEL LOUDON

Housing Project Pumpligahn
Norbert Fritz
Innsbruck, Tyrol, 1986-88,1994-95

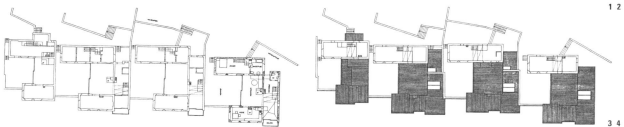

1 2

3 4

This small housing project is located on a terrace of the Inntal valley. Its houses consist of a tower-like front section, a somewhat recessed rear wing, and a construction element connecting the two sections. Together, the three parts enclose an external yard and an inner living space. Rarely does one encounter such a clear division of the elementary housing functions: at the front, a house for cooking and eating; at the back, a house to work in undisturbed or to sleep; in between, spaces of transition and social interaction. The underlying programme is the cell, added together to create a community. What makes this project exciting is the revolutionary combination of materials, building technology and details. Today, simple and proper building is an architectural provocation.

1. General view [photo: A.AZW.]
2. Site plan
3. Apartment level plan
4. Upper level plan

Housing Project Wuhrbaumweg
Mike Loudon, Markus Koch
Bregenz, Vorarlberg, 1988-90

1. Upper level interior
2. From the north
3. Section
[photos: M.S.]

1 2

In the late 1980s, the architecture of residential buildings in Vorarlberg experienced a boost in quantity. The ideas of the Vorarlberg architectural school had finally been accepted in urban architecture and in cooperation projects with large, conventional building contractors. The terraced housing project Wuhrbaumweg features a simple primary structure, offering its occupants a wide variety of floor plans and facades during the planning phase, enabling them to participate actively in the design of details. This was also made possible by the outer wall, which was designed as a modular system of framework rails, allowing panels and casement windows to be positioned according to individual needs. The access corridors which pass before all houses are wide, sunny passages, opening up here and there to informal squares.

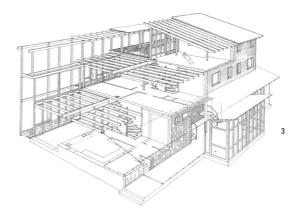

3

Housing Project Im Fang
Dietmar Eberle, Markus Koch, Wolfgang Juen, Norbert Mittersteiner
Höchst, Vorarlberg, 1978-79

1 2

Discontented with their studies, which were rather theoretical and did not provide them with enough practical experience, a group of students from the Austrian province of Vorarlberg, who were studying in Vienna, decided to take matters into their own hands. They wanted to develop an extremely cost-effective residential building project that involved the occupants in the actual construction work and decision-making processes. A simple wooden construction, also understandable by non-experts, was chosen. A covered inner courtyard combines five two- and three-storied houses to form a group. The entrances and the community rooms are located in this area. "Building together, living together" was the motto. The provocative experiment of the housing project "Im Fang" gave rise to the second generation of "Building Artists of Vorarlberg", whose ideas of simplicity and economy have defined a new quality of architecture.

1. Block 3
2. Corridor
[photos: A.L.,K.]

Housing Project Wienerberger Gründe
Ralph Erskine, Hubert Riess
Graz, Styria, 1982–87

1. Path through the housing area [photo: W.K.]
2. Section

Built at the interface between city and countryside, this housing project is a paradigm for the theme "living in the outskirts". The complex offers a balanced combination of empty areas and building volumes. The wide variety of apartment types – a reference to the local building tradition – are accessed through outdoor stairways and pergolas. Together with the light-construction porches, balconies and bay windows, they create a delicate, osmotic layer of communication between indoor and outdoor spaces, a topic that Erskine, in particular, has often considered.

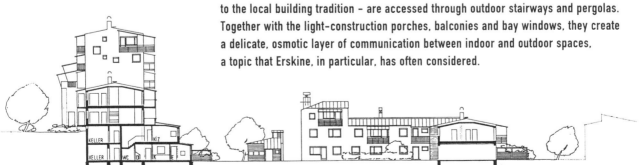

The architect reacts to the inhospitable surroundings of an industrial suburb by exaggerating its potential. On this north/south-aligned tract of land next to a highly frequented thoroughfare, Richter uses a concrete skeleton for the bearing structure, and high-tech glazing on galvanized steel frames for noise protection on the side facing the road. The staircase roofs are made of canvas truck covers and their outer walls consist of laminated wood panels. Containers were employed to accommodate garbage, and used as cellars. The pergolas, separated from the main building structure, are connected to the apartments by transverse bridges. This spatially impressive structure, leading from public to private space, is shielded from the road by a frameless glass wall.

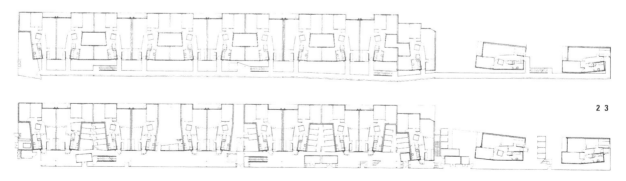

1. Roof terraces with chimneys [photo: M.E.]
2-3. First floor and ground floor plan
3. Night view, glazed exterior corridors [photo: A.Ri.]
4. Frontage [photo: M.E.] pp. 280-281

**Housing
Project
Brunner Strasse**
Helmut Richter
Vienna, 1986–91

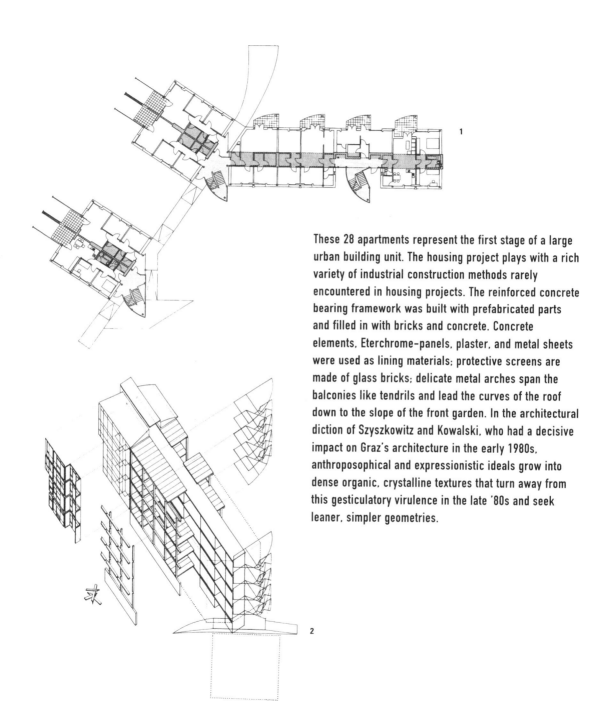

1

These 28 apartments represent the first stage of a large urban building unit. The housing project plays with a rich variety of industrial construction methods rarely encountered in housing projects. The reinforced concrete bearing framework was built with prefabricated parts and filled in with bricks and concrete. Concrete elements, Eterchrome-panels, plaster, and metal sheets were used as lining materials; protective screens are made of glass bricks; delicate metal arches span the balconies like tendrils and lead the curves of the roof down to the slope of the front garden. In the architectural diction of Szyszkowitz and Kowalski, who had a decisive impact on Graz's architecture in the early 1980s, anthroposophical and expressionistic ideals grow into dense organic, crystalline textures that turn away from this gesticulatory virulence in the late '80s and seek leaner, simpler geometries.

2

Housing Project Knittelfeld
Michael Szyszkowitz
Karla Kowalski
Knittelfeld, Styria, 1988-92

1. Ground floor plan
2. Axonometric of the prefabricated building system
3. Building complex, frontage [photo: H.R.]

This terraced house complex with approximately 200 units is located in Vienna's northeastern outskirts. Apart from a busy road on the west side, there was no basis for giving the complex any specific shape. The idea of a garden settlement is implemented in an orthogonal network of paths and alleys, in which three curved east-west rows face each other around an undefined centre. In the north and south, each of the participating architects designed the heads of one of these rows in their own individual manner, leaving their architectural signature. This underlines the overall form, an effect that is again lessened by the colours of Oskar Putz. The entire settlement is characterized by rational order and the play with urban typologies and their concretization.

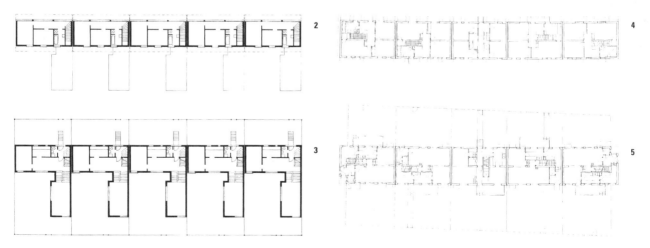

Housing Project Pilotengasse

Adolf Krischanitz
Jacques Herzog & Pierre de Meuron
Otto Steidle + Partners
Vienna, 1989–92

1. Steidle + Partner: duplex town houses
2-3. Herzog & de Meuron: atrium-type, ground floor plan
4-5. Krischanitz, row-buildings, upper level and ground floor plan
6. Herzog & de Meuron: Zweite Zeile (second row) from the west
[photos: M.S.]

This construction is the first part of a larger complex also planned by Wolff-Plottegg. The structural urban plan was preceded by drawing and superimposing reference lines and abstract form data directly on the screen. From this experimental approach, the main axes of the lineaments which were eventually translated into specific systems of ways and building configurations are still perceptible in the final construction. From the construction perspective, the building is expressly serial and reduced: north and south facades in skeleton construction made of prefabricated parts, crosswalls made of brick, minimized supports within the outlines, a hanging steel construction for the horizontal balcony grille on the south side, sheetmetal panelling for the vertical stripes on the northern side, a single window type for the north-or south side.

Housing Project Seiersberg
Manfred Wolff-Plottegg
Graz, Styria, 1987-91

1. From the south
2. Plan
3. From the north, showing stairway
[photos: P.O.]

Large glazed walls and loggias of three apartments on each floor look towards the open west. The longer wing facing the street on the south side features duplexes stacked on top of each other and small apartments on the ground floor. The entrance stairway climbs in a gorge-like space between the two sections up to the planted roof of a hall built in the yard, and to footbridge-like pergolas. The facades are sparingly equipped, with moving blinds in front of the loggias. The loft links the two wings to a single structural unit and covers the monumental portico of the entrance. On several structural levels, the building uniquely demonstrates the dialogue with the city and its cultural context.

1. View from the living room
2. Maisonette wing, street side
[photos: M.S.]

**Apartment Building
Frauenfelderstrasse**
Dieter Henke, Martha Schreieck
Vienna, 1990-93

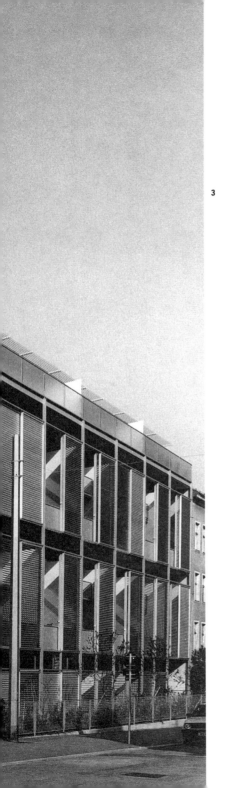

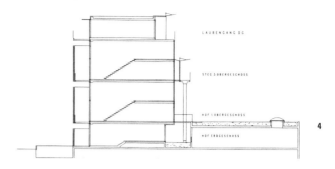

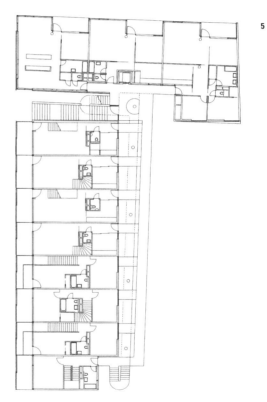

3. General view, from street [photo: M.S.]
4. Section
5. Plan

1

In this low-cost housing project, the architects combined the extreme minimization of material use with an extraordinary optimization of utility value. The floor plan of the connected apartments is divided into three strips. The middle one contains the sanitary units and the kitchen, the lateral strips serve the all other purposes, although as little as possible was done to predetermine their use. The rooms in these apartments are connected by wide sliding or folding doors. Therefore, despite their minimal dimensions, these apartments offer a wide range of possible combinations. All windows extend from the floor to the ceiling. Although there are no balconies, the casements can be opened at an angle of 180 degrees so that each room can be transformed into a loggia.

2

3

Housing Project Strassgang
Florian Riegler
Roger Riewe
Graz, Styria, 1992-94

1. Interior
2. Garden side elevation
3. Plan 50 sq.m. type and 75 sq.m. type
4. Facade with sliding screens
[photos: M.S.]

This is an innovative housing model on the premises of a former coffin factory. The property had been purchased by an association that constructed a boarding house with spacious communal rooms, using the various subsidies offered and financial contributions from its members. The apartments will be rented out and can grow or shrink depending on the life cycles. The bright orange pergola-like sections accommodate approximately 75 units, based on the 45 square metre, two-storey type, separated only by the supply duct and the staircase, easy to combine and separate again. A public café-restaurant with a kitchen for the lodging house, seminar areas, conference hall with a bar, children's centre, indoor swimming pool, and sauna are located in semi-public passages and are accessible to non residents. The roofs are planted with rock gardens and vegetable beds. This is not the place for splendid isolation, but one which allows a view into and through its body and offers room for integrative, urban living.

1. Entrance with café
2. Facade towards street
[photos: H.H.]

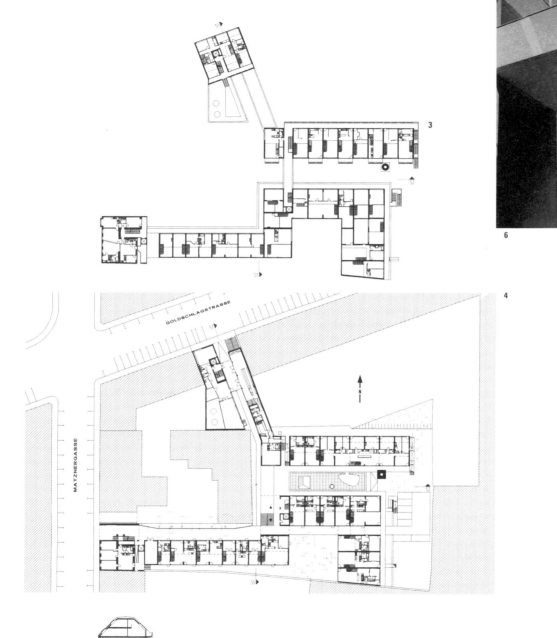

3

4

5

6

3. Third floor plan
4. Ground floor plan
5. Section
6. Building complex, courtyard side
7. Building complex, courtyard side
with stair to indoor swimming pool
[photos: H.H.]

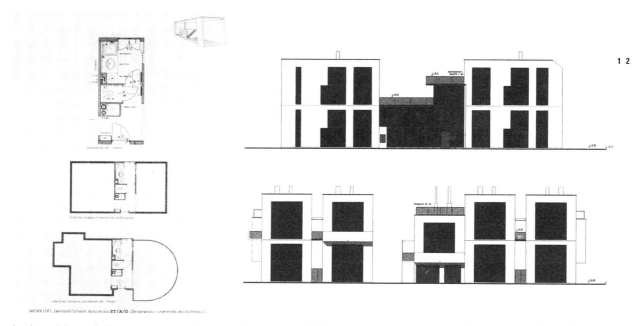

WIENER LOFT, Gerngroß-Schwan, Auszug aus **ST/A/D** „Die generative Grammatik des Wohnhaus"

In view of the exploding costs in social housing, Gerngross & ST/A/D worked on industrial alternatives. The first step in this direction was the "Schnellhaus–Prototyp"(quick house prototype) constructed in 1992 for an exhibition featuring rapid, inexpensive construction concepts for war refugees from former Yugoslavia. The idea of this turnkey, yet "unfinished" structure, which was nevertheless spacious and open to individual enlargement or interior modifications, developed into the "Wiener Loft" patent. The first Viennese loft housing project illustrates the following principles: 17 loft units, two on top of each other, the core of the installation always located in the centre with the staircase, living rooms 4.5 metres high, restrained use of design elements to maximize the available – also vertically illuminated – space. The Viennese loft was inspired by the Domino construction system developed by Le Corbusier in 1914/15.

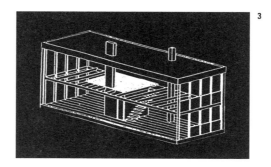

3

"Viennese Loft"
Heidulf Gerngross – Werkstatt Wien
Vienna, 1996–97

1. Expandable sanitary cell of the Viennese loft system
2. Elevation towards Oedenburgerstrasse
3. Axonometric
4. From the east, view from the street [photo: A.K.]

5

5. From the west
6. From the south, courtyard
[photos: A.K.]

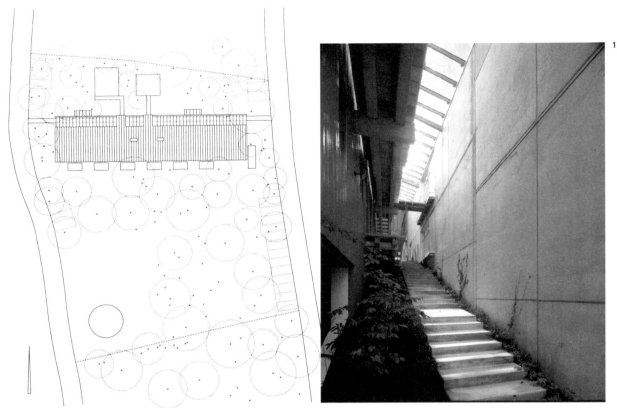

This fairly long construction featuring twelve housing units – ranging from small flats to duplex apartments – is located in the midst of a green area on an inclined tract of land with a thin tree stand.

The building was nicknamed "Roter Laubfrosch" (red tree frog), since the southern side features red wooden weather panelling and large glazed surfaces – windows of up to four metres provide optimum light conditions in every apartment. The path leads from terrace doors to the open natural landscape through wooden footbridges, avoiding the all too habitual delimitation of green space. On the northern side, a glass-covered pathway – bound by vegetation and following the slope of the ground – serves as access and leads to semi-public communication spaces. This housing project by a young team of architects beautifully illustrates that "living in the countryside" does not mean distancing oneself from it but "living together with the countryside".

Housing Project Hödlwald
Splitterwerk
Bürmoos, Salzburg, 1994-96

1. Site plan
2. Corridor
3. General view from the south
[photos: P.O.]

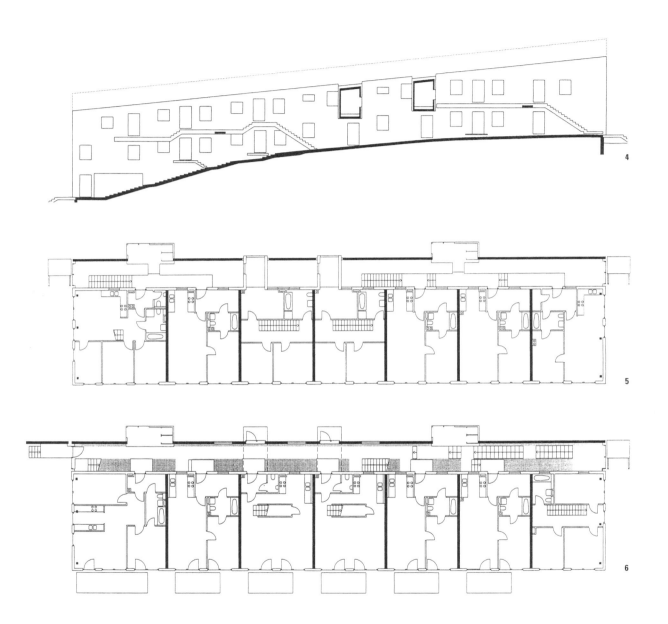

4. Longitudinal section
5. Upper level plan
6. Ground floor plan
7. Detail of the facade [photo: P.O.]

The "Ölzbündt" system combines the advantages of prefabricated wood technology with the maxims of ecological energy optimization and offers affordable single-house elements in a multistorey building for the first time. These 13 housing units were erected in only 18 weeks. The standardized "wooden component system" allows for several variations. Pergolas, balconies and a metal staircase were attached to the facade at specific points only. A regulated hot air heater featuring a geothermic heat exchanger and heat recovery from the exhaust air, as well as a post-heating system using small heat pumps, provide every individual household with heated fresh air. The heating is simultaneously ventilation. This is an elegant and innovative project, and at the same time, cheaper than conventional housing projects.

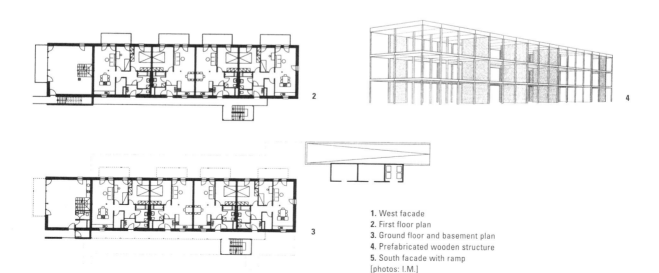

1. West facade
2. First floor plan
3. Ground floor and basement plan
4. Prefabricated wooden structure
5. South facade with ramp
[photos: I.M.]

Housing Project Ölzbündt
Hermann Kaufmann
Dornbirn, Vorarlberg, 1997

Arbeitsgruppe 4 (Team 4)

Clemens Holzmeister's students formed this team
at the Academy of Fine Arts in Vienna in 1950.
MEMBERS Wilhelm Holzbauer, Friedrich Kurrent,
Johannes Spalt, Otto Leitner (until 1953).
MAJOR WORK Church, Parsch, Salzburg, 1953-56; pastoral
centre, Ennsleiten 1958-61; showroom and warehouse
with a building for the O. Anders company, Innsbruck,
1960; St Josef College, Salzburg, Aigen, 1961-64;
presbytery and nursery school, Parsch, Salzburg,
1961-62; Glanzenbichl House, Traunkirchen, Upper
Austria, 1962-64; residential building for Dr B., Vienna,
1963-64; extension of the Residenz Publishing House,
Salzburg, 1964.

ARTEC
Bettina Götz
1962, Bludenz, Vorarlberg.
Richard Manahl
1955, Bludenz, Vorarlberg.
BOTH Studied architecture at the Technical University of
Graz, established the Viennese architectural firm ARTEC
in collaboration with Theo Lang (1985-92) and Ed Hoke
(1987-90); 1993-94 teaching post at the Technical
University of Vienna.
MAJOR WORK Residential and office buildings in Vorarlberg
and Vienna; terraced houses in Weiherweg, Nüziders,
Vorarlberg, 1989-94; residential building Spuller, Vienna,
1990-95; renovation of the court chamber, Leoben,
Styria, 1992-94; residential buildings Wagenredergründe,
Bärnbach, Styria, 1992-95; Kunstraum Wien (exhibition
space), Vienna 1994-96; Zehdengasse Elementary School,
Vienna, 1995-96; Raum (space) Zita Kern, Raasdorf,
Lower Austria, 1997-98.

Othmar Barth
1927, Brixen, South Tyrol (Italy).
1947-52 studied at the Technical University of Graz and
the Technical University of Rome; worked at the Olympic
Planning Centre, Annibale Vitelozzi; since 1955 own
office in Brixen; since 1975 has been teaching at the
Technical University of Innsbruck.
MAJOR WORK Casanus Academy, Brixen, 1960-62;
Lake Hotel Ambach, Bozen, 1970-73; Ski High School,
Stams, 1977-82; diocesan administration centre:
museum, archives and library, Pordenone, 1984-88;
Pastoral Centre, Bozen, 1991-95.

Franz Baumann
1892, Innsbruck, Tyrol — †1974.
Attended the State Trade School in Innsbruck;
from 1918 participation in architecture competitions;
from 1928 freelance architect in Innsbruck.
MAJOR WORK Junior high school, Hotting, Innsbruck
(in collaboration with Siegfried Mazagg); Sport Hotel
Monte Pana, Seiser Alm, South Tyrol; station on the
Nordkettenbahn, funicular railway, Innsbruck (in
collaboration with Siegfried Mazagg), 1927-28; country
house Zach, Reith, 1932; Ortner House on Haydnplatz,
Innsbruck, 1930-32; Mittermayr House, Kössen, 1933-34.

Baumschlager & Eberle
Karl Baumschlager
1956, Bregenz, Vorarlberg.
1975-82 student at the Academy of Applied Arts
in Vienna, professors Hans Hollein (Industrial Design),
O.M. Ungers, Wilhelm Holzbauer; since 1982 freelance
architect; since 1983 cooperation with Dietmar Eberle
in Lochau. Member of the "Gruppe Vorarlberger
Baukünstler", 1994 teaching post at Syracuse University,
New York.
MAJOR WORK Housing development Im Fang, Höchst, 1979
(with Markus Koch and Wolfgang Juen).
Dietmar Eberle
1952, Hittisau (Bregenz Woods), Vorarlberg.
Student of Prof. Anton Schweighofer at the Technical

University of Vienna; study abroad in Iran; 1979–82
member of the "Cooperative" (with Markus Koch,
Norbert Mittersteiner and Wolfgang Juen); since 1983
cooperative with Karl Baumschlager in Lochau;
1982–84 teaching position at the Technical University
of Hannover; since 1985 has been teaching at the
Technical University of Vienna, and at the ETH, Zurich.
Member of the "Gruppe Vorarlberger Baukünstler".
Since 1985 more than 150 realized buildings in
collaboration: housing development, Hohenems
(with D. E., Kurt Egger), 1984-85, Lochau, Tannenbach;
1987-88, Götze House, Dornbirn, 1987; residential
housing development, Lustenau, 1988-90; church hall
Mäder, 1991-95, Vocational Trade School, Bregenz
(in collaboration with Norbert Schweitzer), 1993-94;
Lagertechnik, Wolfurt, 1993-94; Hotel Martinspark,
Dornbirn, 1993-94; reconstruction and extension,
electronics company, Dornbirn, 1994-95; timber
warehouse, Altenried, Germany; presbytery, Satteins,
1995-99; housing development in Innsbruck 1998;
numerous housing developments in Lower Austria,
Tyrol and Vorarlberg.

Peter Behrens
1868, Hamburg (Germany) – †1940 Berlin (Germany).
1886-89 studied painting at the Arts and Crafts school
in Karlsruhe and Düsseldorf; 1893 cofounder of the
Munich Secession; 1903-1907 Director of the Arts and
Crafts School in Düsseldorf; from 1907 artistic councillor
for AEG and independent architect in Berlin; 1922-37
Professor at the Academy of Fine Arts in Vienna;
1936-40 director of the architecture department
at the Prussian Academy of Art in Berlin.
MAJOR WORK Behrens House, Mathildenhöhe, Darmstadt,
1900-1901; AEG Turbine Factory, Moabit, Berlin,
1908-09; AEG high-voltage factory, Berlin, 1909-10;
German Embassy, St Petersburg, 1911-12; administrative
offices for Hoechst AG, Frankfurt, 1920-25; Winarsky-
Hof, Vienna (in collaboration with Josef Frank, Josef
Hoffmann, Oskar Strnad, Oskar Wlach), 1924; residential
housing complex Konstanziagasse, Vienna, 1925;
Franz-Domes-Hof, Vienna, 1928; terraced houses,

Weissenhof, Stuttgart, 1927; office buildings,
Alexanderplatz, Berlin, 1929-30; tobacco factory, Linz,
1929-35 (in collaboration with Alexander Popp).

Ernst Beneder
1958, Waidhofen an der Ybbs, Lower Austria.
1983 graduated from the Technical University of Vienna;
postgraduate student of Prof. Kazuo Shinohara in Tokyo;
1991 taught at the Technical University of Vienna, at
the Tokyo Institute of Technology and at the University
of Illinois; since 1990 freelance architect in Vienna.
Awards and exhibitions in Austria, Japan, Italy, the
Netherlands and USA. 1993 received a promotion award
for the preservation of historical monuments and the
"Golden Trowel" from the state of Lower Austria; 1995
visiting professor at the Technical University of Vienna.
MAJOR WORK G. House, 1991; H. Library, 1991; S. tower
extension, 1992; M. House, 1992; B. House, 1994;
H. House, 1993; urban development project for
Waidhofen an der Ybbs, 1992; City Hall renovation,
Waidhofen an der Ybbs, 1994-1995; Ostarrichi Cultural
Centre in Neuhofen, Lower Austria, 1994-96.

Bétrix & Consolascio
Marie-Claude Bétrix
1953, Neuchâtel (Switzerland).
Studied at the ETH Zurich; 1985-90 lectured
at the School of Engineering in Biel.
Eraldo Consolascio
1948, Locarno (Switzerland).
Studied at the ETH Zurich; 1977 assistant;
1988-90 taught at the ETH Zurich.
1978 founded an architecture office together; 1979-80
worked in collaboration with Fabio Reinhard and Bruno
Reichlin, until 1982 with Bruno Reichlin as well.
MAJOR WORK Trade Building Berani, Uster, 1981-82;
renovation of the Restaurant Hotel des Balances, Luzern
1985; Desulphurization Plant, Salzburg, 1986-87;
single family house, Zurich, 1988; architecture studio,
Erlenbach, 1992; factory, Salzburg, 1986-88;
Umspannwerk Mitte, Salzburg (transformer station),
1992-95; Heizkraftwerk Nord (thermal power station

north) I + II, Salzburg, 1992-95; Heizkraftwerk Mitte (thermal power station), Salzburg, 1986-.

BKK-2
Christoph Lammerhuber
1966, Upper Austria.
Axel Linemayr
1965, Upper Austria.
Florian Wallnöfer
1965, Upper Austria.
Evelyn Wurster
1963, Reutlingen (Germany).
Johann Winter
1949, Vienna.
1993 founded their collective office. Work on several projects and competitions.
MAJOR WORK Loft Factory, Vienna, 1993; student residences, Linz; residential building development in Vienna and Linz 1992-96; office buildings, Vienna, 1992-93; residential building "Sargfabrik" (former coffin factory), Vienna, 1994-96. 1998 Christoph Lammerhuber, Axel Linemayr, Florian Wallnöfer and Evelyn Wurster separate from Johann Winter and established the architecture office pool.

Bily & Katzberger
Karin Bily
1957, Vienna.
Studied at the Technical University of Vienna; since 1978 has shared office with Paul Katzberger.
Paul Katzberger
1957, Vienna.
Studied at the Academy of Fine Arts Vienna; since 1978 has shared office with Karin Bily.
MAJOR WORK Valthe Bookstore; Z. House; N. House; residential building Haberlgasse, Vienna, 1985-89; Lower Austria State Library and State Archives located in the Culture Quarter of St Pölten (in collaboration with Michael Loudon), 1992-97.

Coop Himmelb(l)au
Wolf D. Prix
1942, Vienna.
Studied at the Technical University of Vienna.
Professor at the Academy of Applied Arts in Vienna.
Helmut Swiczinsky
1944, Poznán (Poland).
Studied at the Technical University of Vienna; 1968 established the Coop Himmelb(l)au association; since 1989 offices in Vienna and Los Angeles; numerous assistant professorships in Europe, USA, Japan and Australia; 1988 City of Vienna Architecture Prize; since 1991 Frank Stepper (1955 in Stuttgart) has also been a member of the cooperation.
MAJOR WORK Reiss-Bar, 1977; Baumann Studio, Vienna, 1984-85; renovation of the chanson bar Roter Engel, Vienna, 1980-81; Wahliss-Passage, Vienna, 1985-86; rooftop extension Falkestrasse, Vienna, 1983-88; project to revitalize the Ronacher Theatre in Vienna, 1987; Funderwerk 3, St Veit an d. Glan, Carinthia, 1988; Open House, California, 1989; East Pavilion of the new Museum in Groningen, NL, 1994; Research Centre Seibersdorf, Lower Austria, 1995; Media Pavilion at the Biennale in Venice, 1995; UFA-Cinema Palace, Dresden, 1998; residential sky scraper, Vienna, 1998.
Exhibitions: solo exhibition, Paris, 1992.

Hermann Czech
1936, Vienna.
Student of Prof. Konrad Wachsmann and Ernst A. Plischke. 1974-80 teacher and assistant to Prof. Hans Hollein and Johannes Spalt; 1985 Architecture Prize of the City of Vienna; 1985-86 Visiting Professor at the Academy of Fine Arts in Vienna; 1988-89 and 1993-94 visiting professor at Harvard University in Cambridge (USA); theoretical publications and research papers (on Otto Wagner, Adolf Loos, Josef Frank).
MAJOR WORK Kleines Café (Small Café), Vienna, 1970-74; Wunder-Bar, Vienna 1975-76; subterranean renovation of Schwarzenberg Palace, 1982-84; residential building Petrusgasse, Vienna 1985-89; Stadtparksteg (pedestrian bridge) in the Vienna City Park, 1985-87; residential

building development in Perchtoldsdorf, Lower Austria, 1989-94; elementary school in Simmering, 1993-94; winter glass covering for the Vienna Opera terrace, 1991-94; residential block development Ottakring, Vienna, 1997, renovation of the Bank Austria headquarters building, Vienna, 1997. Design and renovation of numerous cafés in Vienna.

EXHIBITIONS Complete design of the 19th Triennale in Milan, 1995-96.

Günther Domenig

1934, Klagenfurt, Carinthia.

1953-59 studied at the Technical University of Vienna; since 1960 freelance architect; 1969 Grand Prix International d'Urbanisme et d'Architecture in Cannes; 1963-73 partnership with Eilfried Huth; since 1973 own office in Graz; since 1980 professor at the Technical University of Graz; has given numerous lectures and seminars at universities in Europe and in the USA.

MAJOR WORK College of Education, Graz, 1963-69; pastoral centre, Oberwart, 1965-69; research institute and computer centre VÖEST-Alpine, Leoben, (in collaboration with Eilfried Huth), 1969-74; multipurpose hall, Graz, 1974-77; Z-Bank office in Favoriten, Vienna, 1975-79; shipyard, Klagenfurt (in collaboration with Volker Giencke), 1979-82; Humanic shops, 1979-83; extension of the Technical University of Graz, 1983-93; Steinhaus, Steindorf, Carinthia, from 1986; power plant, Unzmarkt (in collaboration with Peter Hellweger), 1988; Z-Bank Austria headquarters, Vienna, 1990-92; State Hospital, Bruck a. d. Mur, 1989-93; Mursteg, Graz, 1992; Carinthia State Exhibition, Hüttenberg, 1995; designed backdrop and costumes for Elektra, Graz Opera House, 1995; Founder, Innovation and Trade Centre, Völkermarkt, 1994-95; Karl-Franzens University Graz, RESOWI Centre, 1994-96; City Museum Leoben, renovation and extension, Styria, 1995-96.

Karl Ehn

1884, Vienna — †1959.

Attended the Academy of Fine Arts in Vienna; 1904-07 studied with Prof. Otto Wagner; 1908-50 worked in the Vienna City Administration, for which he designed communal buildings, especially urban residential buildings, including 2,716 apartments.

MAJOR WORK Bell tower and funeral parlour at the Zentralfriedhof, cemetery, Vienna, 1922-23; housing developments Hermeswiese, Vienna, 1923; Bebelhof, Vienna, 1925-27; Karl-Marx-Hof, Vienna, 1926-30; Adelheid-Popp-Hof, Vienna, 1932; residential buildings Gassergasse, Vienna, 1938, and Wagnergasse, Vienna, 1939; residential buildings and presbytery, Wiedner Hauptsstrasse, Vienna, 1938.

Eichinger or Knechtl
Gregor Eichinger

1956, Wels, Upper Austria.
Studied at the Technical University of Vienna.

Christian Knechtl

1954, Baden, Lower Austria.
Studied at the Technical University of Vienna; since 1985 shared office in Vienna.

MAJOR WORK AND PROJECTS Concept and design for the Austrian entry for the 18th Triennale in Milan, 1992; Café Stein, Vienna, 1985; front page design for the Viennese city paper "Falter", 1986; design for the exhibition "The Salzburg Project", 1986; Stein's Diner, restaurant, Vienna, 1987; design for the exhibition "Birth of a State Capital, St Pölten"; apartment and studio Damisch, Vienna, 1990; interior design for the Helmut Lang stores in Tokyo, Osaka and Paris, 1990; interior design of Haslinger & Keck, Vienna, 1993; reconstruction of the Jewish Museum, Vienna, 1995-96. Erwin-Schrödinger Institute, Vienna, 1996; town square design, Wr. Neustadt, Lower Austria, 1996-97. Design for numerous cafés and shops in Vienna.

Paul Engelmann

1891, Olomouc, Moravia — †1965, Tel Aviv (Israel).
1909 studied at the Technical University of Vienna; attended the Adolf Loos Architecture School; worked in Adolf Loos's office; 1914-18 volunteer during WWI; afterwards freelance architect in Olomouc; 1934 emigration to Israel; 1944-49 published the series

Thoughts (Gedanken); worked for the Israeli newspaper Prozor; on Adolf Loos, Tel-Aviv, 1946; a homage to Karl Kraus, Tel-Aviv, 1949; German edition, Vienna, 1967. PUBLICATIONS Ludwig Wittgenstein Letters. With a Memoir, Oxford, 1967. MAJOR WORK Wittgenstein House, Vienna, 1926-28 (in collaboration with Ludwig Wittgenstein); initiator of the Tourist Club and meeting hall for journalists, Jerusalem; interior design of the throne room, Rabatt Ammon.

Ralph Erskine

1914, London (Great Britain).
Studied in London at the Regent Street Polytechnic; 1938 moved to Sweden and established an office; 1944-45 studied at the Royal Academy of Arts in Stockholm; 1946 opened an office in Drotningholm with Aage Rosenvold from Denmark; 1981 retired from the firm Arken-Erskinearkitekterna A.B. and founded a new firm with Aage Rosenvold, Bengt Ahlquist and Hubert Riess. MAJOR WORK The Box, Lissma, Sweden, 1942; Ski Hotel, Borgafjäll, Sweden, 1948-50; Paper Factory Fors, Avesta, 1950-53; residential housing development Kiruna, 1961-66; residential housing development Resolute Bay, Northwest Territories, Canada, 1973-77; University Frescati, Stockholm, 1974-81; residential housing development Wienerbergergründe, Graz (in collaboration with Hubert Riess) 1982-87; Central Railway Station, Stockholm, 1984-89; office building "The Ark" London, 1988-91.

Max Fabiani

1865, Kobdil (Slovenia) – †1962, Görz.
1883-89 studied at the Technical University of Vienna; 1894-98 worked in Otto Wagner's office, from 1899 office manager; 1902 first architect to write a doctoral thesis at the Technical University of Vienna; 1910-20 professor of design at the Technical University of Vienna; 1917-22 in charge of the reconstruction work in Görz; 1935-1945 mayor of St Daniel in Karst. MAJOR WORK Urban planning for Ljubljana, 1895-1960; commercial building Portois & Fix, Vienna, 1899-1900; residential building Riess, Vienna, 1901-02;

Artaria-Haus, Vienna, 1901-02; Austrian Pavilion International Exhibition Paris, 1901; Slovenian Culture Centre Triest, 1902-05; Urania (observatory and theatre), Vienna, 1909-10; Palais Reithoffer, Vienna, 1912-13; Ursulinenkloster (convent and school), Görz, 1937-39; Villino Gatti, San Trovaso, Venice, 1959.

Max Fellerer

1889, Linz, Upper Austria – †1957, Vienna.
Student of Prof. Karl König at the Technical University of Vienna and of Prof. Josef Hoffmann at the Arts and Crafts School; worked in Hoffmann's studio; assistant at the Academy of Fine Arts in Vienna, 1926-32 worked there with Clemens Holzmeister; 1934-38 Director of the Viennese Arts and Crafts School; 1946-54 Principal of the Academy of Applied Arts, Vienna; 1936-42 and 1945-57 collaborative work with Eugen Wörle. 1945-55 President of the Academy of Applied Arts; 1954 received the Grand Austrian State Prize. MAJOR WORK Handel-Mazzetti-Hof, Linz, 1930; semi-detached building in the Viennese "Werkbundsiedlung", 1930-32; Per-Albin-Hansson residential housing development, Vienna (in collaboration with E. Wörle), 1947-51 and (in collaboration with Pangratz, Schuster, Simony), 1954-55; Gänsehäufel public riverside beach in Vienna (in collaboration with E. Wörle), 1948-50; "Haas House", Vienna (in collaboration with E. Wörle und C. Appel), 1951-52; Concordia-Hof in Vienna (in collaboration with E. Wörle and F. Hasenörl), 1952-58; reconstruction of the Parliament (in collaboration with E. Wörle und C. Appel), 1955-56; extension for the Federal Ministry of Finance, Vienna, 1958-59; terraced building Goldene Stiege (golden stair) Mödling, 1968; Mozarteum (music conservatoire), Salzburg, 1969-72.

Josef Frank

1885, Baden, near Vienna – †1967, Stockholm (Sweden).
Studied at the Technical University of Vienna until 1910. 1914 founding member of the Austrian Werkbund. 1919-25 Professor at the Viennese Arts and Crafts School. 1928 founding member of CIAM; 1934 emigration to Sweden, worked there as a designer for the Svenskt Tenn

company; 1965 Austrian State Prize.

MAJOR BUILDINGS AND FURNITURE DESIGN Scholl House, Vienna, 1914, (in collaboration with Oskar Strnad and Oskar Wlach); residential housing development of the City of Vienna, Hoffingergasse, 1921 (in collaboration with Erich Faber); semi-detatched residential building at the International Werkbund Exhibition in Stuttgart, 1927; Wenzgasse House in Vienna, 1929-30 (in collaboration with Oskar Wlach); building development plan and supervisor for the International "Werkbundsiedlung" in Vienna and the planning of a building, 1930-32; several residential buildings for the City of Vienna (Winarsky-Hof, 1924; Sebastian Kelch Gasse, 1928; Leopoldine-Glöckel-Hof, 1931); upholstery and furniture design.

PUBLICATIONS Architecture as Symbol, Elements of the New German Architecture, 1931; numerous essays.

Konrad Frey

1934, Vienna.
Studied chemistry in Graz and in the USA; afterwards studied architecture at the Technical University of Graz until 1967; 1968-73 worked for ARUP Associates in London and taught at Kingston Polytechnic; established the office Building, Planning & Resources with Florian Beigel; 1973 returned to Graz; studied the possibilities of the use of alternative sources of energy.

MAJOR WORK Kunsthaus (art exhibition hall), Mürzzuschlag, 1988-91; Seggau Congress and Conference Palace, Styria; Fischer House on Grundlsee Lake (in collaboration with Florian Beigl) and Zankel House, Geneva, 1994; Cogeneration Energy Plant, Styria, 1996.

Norbert Fritz

1935, Innsbruck, Tyrol.
Student of Prof. Roland Rainer at the Academy of Fine Arts; since 1970 own office in Innsbruck.

MAJOR WORK House in Tabadill; Reith Cemetery, Alpachtal; House in Schwarzach St Veit; sculpture studio in Hatting, Tyrol; local government building in Strass, Zillertal; Ötz Cemetery, Ötztal; residential housing development Pumpligahn, Innsbruck, 1988-95.

Gerhard Garstenauer

1925, Futsch an der Glocknerstrasse, Salzburg.
1947-52 studied at the Technical University of Vienna and at Siegfried Theiss's School; since 1954 freelance architect in Salzburg; taught at the University of Innsbruck 1973-78.

MAJOR WORK ÖFAG, Salzburg, 1958; Felsenbad (bath house), Badgastein, Salzburg 1967-68; commercial building Ford Schmidt, Salzburg, 1972; sports centre, Badgastein,1974; Solarbad (solar bath house) Dorfgastein, Salzburg 1978.

Heidulf Gerngroß

1939, Carinthia.
Originally a carpenter; 1958-61 studied architecture at the Technical University of Vienna; 1961-62 study abroad in Tokyo; 1968-71 post graduate studies at the University of California, Los Angeles; since 1965 has worked in collaboration with Helmut Richter; 1977 established an office together.

MAJOR WORK P. House, Wiener Neustadt, 1978-89 (in collaboration with Helmut Richter); Königseder House, Upper Austria, 1980 (in collaboration with Helmut Richter).

INDEPENDENT WORK Design of the "Viennese Loft", derived from the "S/T/A/D – Schnellhaus", 1993; residential housing development Wiethestrasse, 1994; first Viennese loft housing development, Vienna, 1996-97; Friedrich Kiesler School, Vienna, 1998.

Volker Giencke

1947, Wolfsberg, Carinthia.
Studied architecture and philosophy in Vienna and Graz; 1974-78 worked with Günther Domenig and Eilfried Huth; since 1981 independent architect in Vienna; Professor at the University of Innsbruck and at Yale University.

MAJOR WORK Shipyard at Wörthersee Lake, Klagenfurt, 1979-82 (in collaboration with Günther Domenig); single family houses in Graz; greenhouse for the Botanical Institute at the University of Graz, 1982-93; showroom, office and storage building for a wholesale sanitation company, Klagenfurt, 1989-90; Church Aigen in Ennstal, Styria, 1985-92; Austrian Pavilion at the EXPO 92, Seville; athletic hall, Graz, 1987-93; housing development Carl-Spitzweg-Gasse, Graz, 1992-93; Hotel Speicher, Barth, Germany, 1995-97.

Roland Gnaiger

1951, Bregenz, Vorarlberg.
Student of Prof. Ernst A. Plischke, Gustav Peichl and Roland Rainer at the Academy of Fine Arts in Vienna and at the Technical University of Eindhoven (Netherlands); since 1979 offices in Bregenz and Doren; teaches design at the Faculty of Architecture at the University of Innsbruck. Member of the "Gruppe Vorarlberger Baukünstler".
MAJOR WORK Single family houses; Elsässer House, Bregenz, 1981-82; Zadra House, Lustenau, 1987-88; Grabherr House, Lustenau, 1988; Ladstätter House, Bregenz, 1990; housing development Franz-Michael-Felder-Hof, Hohenems, 1982-83; terraced house complex Moosmahd-strasse, Wolfurt, 1985-86; theatre, Doren, 1990; elementary school Worth, 1990/92; event and conference room at the Bregenz High School, 1990-91; school, Warth, Vorarlberg, 1991-92; conversion of the Villa Heimann-Rosenthal into the Jewish Museum Hohenems, (museographic design Elsa Prochazka), 1988-91; organic farm Vetterhof, Lustenau, Vorarlberg, 1995-96.

Johann Georg Gsteu

1927, Hall, Tyrol.
Graduated from the Arts and Crafts School, department of sculpture; 1950-53 student of Prof. Clemens Holzmeister at the Academy of Fine Arts in Vienna; since 1958 freelance architect; 1968 State Price for architecture, professor for architecture and design at the Polytechnic in Kassel.
MAJOR WORK Renovation of the Rosenkranzkirche church, 1956-58 (in collaboration with Friedrich Achleitner), and parish hall, Vienna, 1968-71; priests' centre, Vienna, 1960-65; housing for sculptors, St Margarethen, Burgenland, 1962-68; priests' centre Steyr-Ennsleiten, 1968-70 (in collaboration with Team 4); Josef-Bohmann-Hof, Vienna, 1973; part of the residential complex Aderklaaerstrasse, Vienna, 1973-78; Park & Ride Siebenhirten, Vienna, 1995; nursery school and day care centre, Vienna, 1994-95; underground stations in Vienna, 1991-96; north walkway over the Danube, Vienna, 1994-97.

Oswald Haerdtl

1899, Vienna – †1959.
1919-21 student of Prof. Oskar Strnad at the Arts and Crafts School in Vienna; 1922-30 assistant in Josef Hoffmann's studio; from 1935 responsible for the special architecture programme at the Arts and Crafts School; from 1939 own studio; after 1945 responsible for the architecture programme at the Academy of Applied Arts in Vienna.
MAJOR WORK Confectionery Altmann & Kühne, Vienna, 1932 (in collaboration with Josef Hoffmann); semi-detatched building in the Viennese "Werkbundsiedlung", 1932; Austrian Pavilion, World Fair Brussels, 1935 and Paris, 1937; Federal Chancellor's Building, Vienna, 1948; office building Mahlerstrasse 6, Vienna, 1949; Espresso Arabia, Vienna, 1950; office building at the corner of Singerstrasse and Kärntnerstrasse, Vienna, 1953; Volksgarten dance-café, Vienna, 1954-58; fair pavilion Felten & Guillaume, Vienna, 1954; Café Prückel, Vienna, 1955; Mierka House, Salzburg, 1957; City of Vienna's Historical Museum, 1954-59.

Bernhard Hafner

1940, Graz, Styria.
Studied architecture at the Technical University of Graz, graduated in 1965; 1967 Master's degree in architecture at Harvard University; 1968-79 taught at the University of California, Cornell University and at the University of Texas; 1979 returned to Austria.
MAJOR WORK Government office building Krakaudorf 1, 1981; government office building Krakaudorf 2, 1982; residential housing development Grabenschlössl, Graz, 1983-90; residential housing development Rettenbach, 1990-92; laboratory building of the Montan University, Leoben, 1992; residential housing development Andritzer Reichsstrasse, Graz, 1994.

Otto Häuselmayer

1943, Vienna.
Studied at the Technical University of Vienna and at
the Summer Academy in Salzburg in the workshop of
J.B. Bakema; 1969-77 worked at the Wilhelm Holzbauer
atelier; since 1977 own office in Vienna.
MAJOR WORK Main planning of the urban development project
at Wienerberggelände, Vienna, 1978-95; surface design
of the Freyung city plaza in Vienna, 1988-89;
residential housing Biberhaufenweg, Vienna, 1981-85
(in collaboration with Heinz Tesar, Carl Pruscha);
residential housing Adambergergasse, Vienna, 1987-92;
residential housing Pappenheimgasse, Vienna, 1991-93;
residential housing at the Herzgründe, Vienna, 1991-93;
church and parish hall Emmaus am Wienerberg, Vienna,
1991-92; residential housing development in
Süssenbrunn, Vienna; Zu den Heiligen Cyrill und Method
Church, Vienna, 1992-95; residential and commercial
building, Vienna, 1995-97.

Henke & Schreieck
Dieter Henke

1952, Kössen, Tyrol.
Studied at the Academy of Fine Arts with Prof. Roland
Rainer 1973-80; afterwards assistant at the Institute for
Urban Planning at the Academy; various studies abroad
in Africa, Asia and the USA.

Martha Schreieck

1954, Innsbruck, Tyrol.
1975-81 student of Prof. Roland Rainer and Timo
Penttilä at the Academy of Fine Arts; studies abroad
in Asia and in the USA; since 1983 has shared office
with Dieter Henke; 1993 taught at the Technical
University in Innsbruck; 1995 Visiting Professor
at the Academy of Fine Arts in Vienna.
MAJOR WORK Single family houses and apartment
rennovation, 1982-90; Penthouse, Landstrasse Vienna,
1986; residential buildings in Klosterneuburg, 1985,
Liesing Vienna, 1986, and Landeck, Tyrol, 1992;
residential housing complex Frauenfelderstrasse, Hernals,
Vienna, 1990-93; Department of Social and Economic
Studies, Innsbruck, 1989-98; adaption of the Hackinger

pedestrian walkway in Meidling, Vienna, 1992-94
(in collaboration with W.D. Ziesel); Leberberg School,
Vienna, 1994-96; terraced residental housing development
Seefeld, Tyrol, 1994-95; residential building project
Steinergasse, Vienna, 1995-.

Jacques Herzog & Pierre de Meuron

Both 1950, Basel (Switzerland).
Both studied at and graduated from the ETH Zurich;
since 1978 Herzog & de Meuron office in Basel; 1984
visiting professor at Cornell University, New York State;
1987 received the Art Award from the Academy of Arts,
Berlin; 1989 Visiting Professor at Harvard University,
Cambridge, and 1991 at Tulane University, New Orleans.
MAJOR WORK Blue House, Oberwil, Basel, 1979-80; Photo
Studio Frei, Weil, 1980-81; stone house, Tavole, Italy,
1982-88; plywood house, Bottmingen, Basel, 1984-85;
building alongside a dividing wall, Basel, 1984-88;
Schwitter House, Basel, 1985-88; SBB signal box 4,
Basel, 1987-94; worked on the residential housing
development Pilotengasse, Vienna, 1989-92
(in collaboration with Krischanitz and Steidle); building
for a collection of contemporary art, Munich, 1990-92;
student residences, Antipodes I, Dijon, France, 1990-92
(in collaboration with Rémy Zaugg); renovation of
the SUVA building Basel, 1991-93; Ricola warehouse,
Laufen, Switzerland; SBB signal box 4, Basel, 1992-95.

Thomas Herzog

1941, Munich (Germany).
Architectural studies and Diploma at the Technical
University, Munich until 1965; 1965-69 collaboration
with Prof. Peter C. von Seidlein, Munich; 1969-72
assistant at the University of Stuttgart; since 1972 in
private practice in collaboration with Verena Herzog-
Loibl (designing of building systems using renewable
energies); since 1974 Professor at various universities
(Kassel, Darmstadt and Munich); Visiting Professor
at the Ecole Polytechnique Féderale, Lausanne.
Since 1994 partnership with Hans Jörg Schrade.
MAJOR WORK Since 1977 many residential housing
developments and private houses in Germany;

building systems for passive solar energy houses in Sulmona, Italy, 1983-85 convention and exhibition centre (Designcentre), Linz, 1988-93; Hotel, Linz, 1988-93; office building, Wiesbaden (Germany), 1994-; residential building, Linz, 1994-; office building, Hanover (Germany), 1996-.

Margarethe Heubacher-Sentobe

1945, Schwaz, Tyrol.
1966-70 student of Prof. Rainer at the Academy of Fine Arts in Vienna; assisted and worked in architectual offices in Innsbruck; built several single family houses; since 1978 own office in Schwaz; since 1991 has been teaching at the University in Innsbruck.
MAJOR WORK Numerous single family houses in Tyrol; two residential housing developments in Schwaz, Tyrol; residential housing development in Wörgl, Tyrol; senior citizens' clubhouse and city park landscaping, Schwaz, Tyrol; Kindergarten, Zell am Ziller; Wanitschek House Brixlegg, Tyrol, 1993-94; studio for a musician, Weerberg, Tyrol, 1995-96.

Ernst Hiesmayr

1920, Innsbruck, Tyrol.
Studied at the Technical University of Graz until 1948; since 1948 own offices in Innsbruck, Vienna and Wolfurt; 1967 dissertation on the revitalization of residential buildings; 1968-90 Professor at the Technical University of Vienna (1975-77 Principal); 1975 Architecture Prize from the City of Vienna.
MAJOR WORK Junior high school in Bregenz, 1950; Chamber of Commerce Vorarlberg, Bregenz, 1951; Clima Hotels in Vienna and Innsbruck, 1959; priests' complex in Linz, 1961-67; Villa Hotel Bockkeller, Vienna, 1963-65; Parisini studio building, Neusiedl am Steinfelde, 1964; Institute for Economic Development Dornbirn, 1967; Dr Siemer House, Wachau-Gosam, 1968; law department, university building, Vienna, 1968-84; Honeywell office building, Vienna, 1971; Dr Lanner House, Vienna, 1973-75; Gewerbehof (business park), Vienna, 1985; Giro Bank headquarters renovation, Schubertring 5, Vienna, 1985.

Josef Hoffmann

1870, Pirnitz, Moravia — †1956, Vienna.
1892-95 student of Prof. Karl von Hasenauer and Otto Wagner at the Academy of Fine Arts in Vienna, then worked in Wagner's studio; 1898 co-founder of the Viennese Secession; 1899-1937 professorship at the Arts and Crafts School in Vienna; 1903 founded the Viennese "Werkstätte" in collaboration with Kolo Moser and Fritz Waerndorfer; 1912 cofounded the Austrian "Werkbund"; designer; received many awards in Austria and abroad, including the Austrian State Prize in 1950.
MAJOR WORK Sanatorium Purkersdorf near Vienna, 1904; Palais Stoclet, Brussels, 1905-11; residential building Skywa-Primavesi, Vienna, 1913-15; Austria House at the German "Werkbund" Exhibition, Cologne, 1914; a section of the residential housing complex Winarsky-Hof, Vienna, 1924-25; residential building Sonja Knios, Vienna, 1924-25; terraced houses in the Viennese "Werkbundsiedlung", 1932; Austrian Pavilion for the International Arts and Crafts Exhibition, Paris, 1925; and for the Biennale, Venice, 1934.

Hans Hollein

1934, Vienna.
Student of Prof. Clemens Holzmeister at the Academy of Fine Arts in Vienna until 1956; 1958-64 studied at the IIT Chicago and at the University of California, Berkeley; since 1964 own office in Vienna; 1967-76 professor at the Academy of Fine Arts in Düsseldorf and since 1976 at the Academy of Applied Arts in Vienna. 1966 and 1984 Reynolds Memorial Award, 1979 Bard Award, 1974 City of Vienna Architecture Prize, 1983 Grand Austrian State Prize, 1985 received the Pritzker Architecture Prize.
MAJOR WORK Retti candle store, Vienna, 1964-65; Richard Feigen Gallery, New York, 1969; interior design for Siemens AG, Munich, 1970-75; Schullin jewelers I, 1972-74 and II, 1984, Vienna; Köhlergasse Elementary School, Vienna, 1977-90; Österreichisches Verkehrsbüro (travel agency), Vienna, 1980; Mönchengladbach City Museum, Germany, 1972-82; Museum of Modern Art Frankfurt/Main, 1983-91; Haas House, Vienna, 1985-90;

project for the Guggenheim Museum in Salzburg, 1990 and in Vienna, 1993-94; museum and exhibition hall, Cultural Quarter St Pölten, 1992-99; bank in Madrid, 1994; Volcano Museum, France, 1994-; elementary school, Danube City, Vienna, 1990-99; Zumtobel-Lichtforum showroom in Vienna, 1995-96.

Wilhelm Holzbauer

1930, Salzburg.
1950-53 studied in Clemens Holzmeister's master class at the Academy of Fine Arts in Vienna; 1956-57 studied at M.I.T. in Cambridge; 1957-59 Visiting Professor in Canada and in the USA; until 1964 member of Team 4 (with Johannes Spalt and Friedrich Kurrent); from 1964 own office in Vienna; since 1977 Professor at the Academy of Applied Arts in Vienna; numerous international prizes and awards of recognition.
BUILDINGS See Team 4.
INDEPENDENT WORK Residential housing complex "living tomorrow", Vienna, 1973-79; Vorarlberg State Government House, Bregenz (in collaboration with Mätzler, Schweitzer, Rapf) 1975-81; City Hall and Opera House, Amsterdam (in collaboration with Dam, Bijovet en Holt), 1969-86; interior design of subway stations in Vienna (in collaboration with Heinz Marschalek, Georg Ladstätter, Bert Gantar), since 1973; natural sciences department building at the University of Salzburg (in collaboration with Ekhart, Hübner, Ladstätter, Marschalek), 1978-86; office building complex, Vienna (in collaboration with Glück, Hlaweniczka, Lintl, Lippert), 1978-94; Center for Biology at the Univisity of Frankfurt/Main (in collaboration with Mayr), 1988-93; Diplomatic Centre, Danube City, Vienna, 1990; Kärntnerringhof, Vienna (in collaboration with Lippert), 1990-93; Bank Austria offices, Vienna, (in collaboration with Hlawenizcka, Lintl, Glück und Lippert),1993-94; Andromeda Tower, Danube City, Vienna, 1993-1997; Austrian National Bank, extension, Vienna, 1997.

Clemens Holzmeister

1886, Fulpmes, Tyrol – †1983, Salzburg.
Student of Prof. M. Ferstel; L. Simony and C. König at the Technical University of Vienna; 1919-24 assistant; 1924-28 Professor at the Academy of Fine Arts in Vienna; 1928-32 responsible for the architecture programme at the Academy of Art in Düsseldorf; 1934 Austrian federal councillor for art; 1938-1945 lived in Turkey, from 1940-49 Professor at the Technical University of Istanbul; 1953 Grand Austrian State Prize; 1954-1957 Professor at the Viennese Academy of Fine Arts.
MAJOR WORK St Johannes Church, Batschuns, 1921-23; Mariahilf Church, Bregenz, 1921-31; crematorium, Vienna, 1921-22; Blathof, Vienna, 1924-25; festival theatre in Salzburg, 1926; Trinkhalle (pump room), Bad Hall, 1927; government buildings in Ankara, 1927-42; "Akademikerhilfe" student residences, Vienna, 1931-32; Kanzlerkirche, church, Vienna, 1933; terraced houses in the Viennese "Werkbundsiedlung", 1932; Neuland School, Vienna, 1933; new festival theatre in Salzburg, 1960; St Johann Church, Volders, Tyrol, 1965.

Wolfgang Juen

1952, Matrei am Brenner, Tyrol.
Attended a polytechnic high school specializing in structural engineering in Innsbruck; studied at the Academy of Fine Arts Vienna; 1979–82 worked in the Cooperative; own office in Dornbirn; member of the "Gruppe Vorarlberger Baukünstler".
MAJOR WORK Residential housing development Im Fang, Höchst (in collaboration with Dietmar Eberle and Markus Koch), 1979; residential housing development Nachtgärtle, Fussach, 1983-84.

Jabornegg & Pálffy
Christian Jabornegg

1956, Wels, Upper Austria.
András Pálffy

1954, Budapest (Hungary).
Office together since 1988.
MAJOR WORK Exhibition halls for contemporary art, renovation and extension of the Generali Foundation, Vienna, 1993-95; renovation of the south wing of the central railway station in Kassel for documenta X, 1997; Fridericianum, exhibition rooms for contemporary art,

temporary rebuilding, documenta X, 1997; renovation and extension of the Schoeller Bank, Vienna, 1998-; Archeological Museum at Judenplatz, renovation and extension of the exhibition rooms for the mediaeval archaeological findings, Vienna, (during the construction of the memorial designed by Rachel Whiteread), 1996-.

Klaus Kada

1940, Leibnitz near Graz, Styria.
1961-71 studied at the Technical University of Graz; 1976 founded his own office in Leibnitz.
MAJOR WORK Kada department store, Leibnitz, 1972-73; Sparkasse, bank Bad Radkersburg (in collaboration with G. Lauffer), 1977-80; residential housing development Mitterling, Bad Radkersburg, 1978-82; land surveying office, Leibnitz, 1988; Glass Museum, Bärnbach, Styria, 1987-88; Tögl House, Graz, 1990-92; research and development centre for Leykam-Mürztaler-AG, Gratkorn, 1990-91; student residence, Graz, 1988-92; senior citizens' home, Leibnitz, 1993-95; festival theatre, St Pölten, 1994-97; extension of Karl Franzens University, Graz, 1994-97.

Kastner & Waage
Eugen Kastner
1897 − †1945.
Fritz Waage
1898, Ilok − †1968, Vienna.
Studied at the Technical University of Vienna; from 1923 worked in Hubert Gessner's studio; independent architect in Vienna; until 1945 collaborative work with Eugen Kastner; afterwards with Wilhelm Kroupa.
MAJOR WORK Transformer Station 3, Vienna, 1928-30; Dorotheum (auction room) Währing, Vienna (in collaboration with Wilhelm Kroupa), 1931; Transformer Station 10, Vienna, 1928-31; portal of the Austrobus Travel Agency, Vienna, around 1937; rebuilding of the building "Zu den vier Jahreszeiten" (the four seasons), 1937; Soccer House, Vienna, 1954 (in collaboration with Wilhelm Kroupa).

Hermann Kaufmann

1955, Reuthe, Vorarlberg.
1975-81 studied in Innsbruck and Vienna; worked in Ernst Hiesmayr's office; since 1983 own architecture office in partnership with Elmar Gmeiner and Christian Lenz.
MAJOR WORK Organ Factory, Schwarzach, Vorarlberg; production and warehouse for Kaufmann Holzbauwerk (timber plant), Reuthe, Vorarlberg, 1992; furniture factory, Kaltbrunn, Switzerland, 1993; seminar house St Arbogast; solar school, Dafins.

Leopold Kaufmann

1932, Reuthe, Vorarlberg.
Studied carpentry and attended the Polytechnic High School for Structural Engineering in Innsbruck; 1955-60 studied at the Technical University of Graz; since 1965 own office in Dornbirn.
Has realized about 140 works of architecture.
MAJOR WORK Rüfikopfbahn, railway, Lech am Arlberg, 1987-88; Karrenseilbahn, cable car and restaurant, Dornbirn, 1995-96, Golmerbahn, railway, Vadans, 1995.

Markus Koch

1952, Feldkirch, Vorarlberg.
Studied at the Academy of Fine Arts in Vienna; 1979–82 worked in the Cooperative; since 1987 own office in Feldkirch. Member of the "Gruppe Vorarlberg Baukünstler"; assistant to Prof. A. Henz at the ETH Zurich.
MAJOR WORK Housing development Im Fang, Höchst, 1979 (in collaboration with Dietmar Eberle and Wolfgang Juen); house in Altach, 1982; housing development In der Emme, Altach, 1984-85; terraced house complex Sulz, 1989; housing development Wuhrbaumweg, Bregenz (in collaboration with Michael Loudon), 1988-90; multipurpose hall Schlins, (in collaboration with Michael Loudon), 1988-90; housing development Wiesenbach, Schlins (with Michael Loudon), 1990-92.

Manfred Kovatsch

1940, Villach.
Studied at the Technical University of Graz and 1970-71

at the University of California, Berkley; 1972 assistant
at the Technical University of Munich; from 1975
taught at the Technical University of Graz; since 1986
Professor at the Munich Academy of Fine Arts.
MAJOR WORK Lakeside house, Ossiach, Carinthia, 1975-77;
construction company, Carinthia, 1979; bakery with
three ovens, Villach, 1982; residential housing, Munich
1984; residential housing complex, Munich-Puchheim,
1986; residential building, Graz, 1988.

Adolf Krischanitz

1946, Schwarzach.
1965-72 studied at the Technical University of Vienna;
1970 cofounder of the group Missing Link (with Angela
Hareiter and Otto Kapfinger); 1991 City of Vienna
Architecture Prize and participation in the 5th
Architecture Biennale in Venice; 1991-1995 president
of the Viennese Secession; since 1992 professor at the
Academy of Arts in Berlin.
MAJOR WORK Renovated the Viennese "Werkbundsiedlung",
1983, and the Viennese Secession, 1986; Kuoni travel
agency, Vienna (with Otto Kapfinger), 1984; residential
housing development Forellenweg, Salzburg, 1986-90;
housing development Pilotengasse, Vienna (in
collaboration with Steidle and Herzog & de Meuron),
1989-92; exhibition pavilion at Traisen, St Pölten, 1988;
commercial and office buildings, Schillerpark, Linz 1989-
94; Kunsthalle (art exhibition hall), Vienna, 1991-92;
Neue Welt School, Vienna, 1992-94; Kunsthalle, Krems,
1993-95; master plan for the Danube City, Vienna
(in collaboration with Heinz Neumann), 1990; renovated
headquarters of the Vienna Post Office (in collaboration
with Heinz Neumann), 1994; numerous single family
houses and furniture designs.

Friedrich Kurrent

1931, Salzburg.
Studied at the State Trade School in Salzburg and at the
Academy of Fine Arts in Vienna under Prof. Clemens
Holzmeister; 1952-64 member of Team 4 (with Johannes
Spalt and Wilhelm Holzbauer); 1965 founding member
of the Austrian Architecture Society; 1968-71 assistant
to Prof. E.A. Plischke at the Academy of Fine Arts in
Vienna; since 1973 Professor at the Technical University
of Munich; 1979 City of Vienna Architecture Prize; 1981-
83 Dean of the architecture department at the Technical
University of Munich; 1997 received the "Austrian
Honourable Cross for Science and Arts 1st Class".
BUILDINGS See Team 4.
INDEPENDENT WORK Bergkapelle, chapel, Murau, Styria, 1991;
Protestant church in Aschheim near Munich,
Germany,1996; Catholic church in Kirchham, Upper
Austria, 1997/98.

Josef Lackner

1911, Wörgl, Tyrol.
Student of Prof. Clemens Holzmeister at the Academy
of Fine Arts in Vienna until 1952; worked in many
architectural offices in Düsseldorf, Freiburg and Munich;
since 1961 own office in Innsbruck; 1977 received the
"Award of Honour for Fine Arts" from the Ministry of
Art and Science, since 1979 professor at the Technical
University of Innsbruck.
MAJOR WORK Neu-Arzel Church, Innsbruck, 1959; Sigmund
Kripp House, Innsbruck, 1964; Konzils-Gedächtnis-Kirche
church, Lainz, Vienna, 1965-68; Völs Church, Innsbruck,
1967; presbytery Glanzing, Vienna, 1968;
Ursulinenkloster: school, residences and convent church,
Innsbruck, 1971; Lichtstudio Bartenbach, Tyrol, 1988;
office building, Salzburg, 1989-92; office building and
working hall for the Jenbacher Werke factory, Tyrol,
1992-93.

Rüdiger Lainer

1949, Kaprun, Salzburg.
Studied physics, painting and sociology in Vienna and
Paris; studied architecture at the Technical University of
Vienna; research work on urban sociology; since 1985
own office in Vienna; since 1983 collaborative work
with Gertraud Auer; 1989 together with Gertraud Auer
Visiting Professor in Buenos Aires, Argentina.
Buildings in collaboration with Gertraud Auer:
residential housing development Engerthstrasse, Vienna;
residential building Gyrowetzgasse, Vienna, 1985-88;

residential building Waidhausenstrasse, Vienna, 1987-90; renovation of the residential building Hermanngasse, Vienna, 1990.

INDEPENDENT WORK Absberggasse junior high school, Vienna, 1993-94; penthouse loft extension, Vienna, 1994-95; renovation of Palais Equitable, Vienna, 1996-97; cinema and shopping centre Eurocity, Salzburg, 1997-99.

Adolf Loos

1870, Brno − †1933, Vienna.
1890-93 studied at the Technical University of Dresden; visited the United States (Chicago, Philadelphia and New York); 1896 established an architectural office in Vienna; journalist for the newspaper "Neue freie Presse", from 1903 publisher of the magazine "Das Andere - Ein Blatt zur Einfuehrung abendlaendischer Kultur in Oesterreich"; 1912-13 founding of the Loos-Bauschule (Loos School for Architecture); 1920 general architectural plan for Vienna (with Peter Behrens, Josef Frank, Josef Hoffmann and Oskar Strnad); 1921-24 chief architect of the Bureau for Housing of the City of Vienna; 1924-28 lived and worked in Paris.

PUBLICATIONS Ornament und Verbrechen (Ornament and Criminality), Vienna 1908; Richtlinien für ein Kunstamt (Guidelines for a Bureau of Arts), Vienna 1919; Ins Leere gesprochen (Spoken into Emptiness), Zurich 1921; Trotzdem (Despite the Fact), Innsbruck 1931

MAJOR WORK Café Museum, Vienna, 1899; renovation of the Villa Karma, Clarens, Montreux, 1903-06; Kärntner-Bar, Vienna, 1908; Steiner House, Vienna, 1910; commercial and residential building Goldman & Salatsch, Vienna 1909-11; Leopold Goldman House, Vienna 1909-11; Salon Knize, Vienna, 1910-13; Stoessl House, Vienna 1911-12; Horner House, Vienna, 1912; Scheu House, Vienna 1912-13; Manz bookshop, Vienna, 1912; Café Capua, Vienna, 1913; Mandl House, Vienna 1916; Villa Strasser, Vienna, 1918-19; Heuberg housing development, Vienna 1921-24; houses for the residential development "Kriegerheim-siedlung" Hirschstetten, Vienna, 1921; Herrensalon Mandl, Vienna, 1923; Tristan Tzara House, Paris, 1925-26; Moller House, Vienna, 1927-28; Brummel House, Plzen, 1928-29; Müller House, Prague, 1928-30;

two semi-detached houses in the Viennese "Werkbund-siedlung" (in collaboration with Heinrich Kulka), 1932.

Michael Loudon

1950, Nebraska (USA).
Student of Prof. Gustav Peichl at the Academy of Fine Arts in Vienna; since 1987 own office in Feldkirch (with Markus Koch) and Vienna.

MAJOR WORK Housing developments Bregenz, 1989-90, and Schlins, 1990-92; a multipurpose building in Schlins (in collaboration with Markus Koch), 1988-90; housing development Wuhrbaumweg, Bregenz (in collaboration with Markus Koch), 1988-90; single family residence, Lochau, 1989; residential building Leflergasse, Vienna; residential housing development Erzherzog Karl Stadt, Vienna; State Library and State Archives in the Culture Quarter of St Pölten (in collaboration with Paul Katzberger and Karin Bily), 1992-97; residential building in Vienna's Danube City, 1990-.

Luger & Maul
Maximilian Luger

1958, Kleinzell, Upper Austria.
Studied at the Technical University of Vienna, at the University of Applied Arts in Vienna, and at the University of Art and Industrial Design, Linz; since 1988 own office in Wels, Upper Austria; since 1989 collaborative work with Franz Maul; teaching at the Fachhochschule Rosenheim.

Franz Maul

1954, Nussdorf am Attersee.
Studied at the University of Art and Industrial Design in Linz; since 1985 independent architect in Wels; since 1989 collaborative work with Maximilian Luger.

MAJOR WORK Commercial building Heiter in Schwanenstadt; renovation of the Raiffeisenbank, Wels; Seebad Häupl am Attersee (public swimming area on Lake Attersee), Upper Austria, 1990-91; City Hall Wels; Kulturzentrum (Cultural Centre) St Gallen; bathing area and lake camping ground at Lake Attersee, Upper Austria, 1996-97; hairdressing salon, Linz, 1997.

Fritz Gerhard Mayr

1931, Raab, Upper Austria.

1954-57 student of Prof. Lois Welzenbacher and Roland Rainer at the Academy of Fine Arts in Vienna; worked in the offices of Roland Rainer and Wilhelm Hubatsch; freelance architect in Vienna.

MAJOR WORK Modellschule, Wörgl, Tyrol, 1974 (in collaboration with Viktor Hufnagl); Church "Zur heiligsten Dreifaltigkeit" (of the Holy Trinity), Vienna (in collaboration with Fritz Wotruba), 1965-76; boarding school St Berthold, Wels, Upper Austria, 1976; junior school Raab, Upper Austria, 1978; Verkehrsbüro, travel agency, Vienna, 1979-80.

Meili & Peter
Marcel Meili

1953, Küsnacht/Zurich (Switzerland).

1973-80 Student of Aldo Rossi and Mario Campi at the Federal Institute of Technology (ETH), Zurich; 1973-80 thesis project and subsequent work in offices of Prof. Schnebli; 1981-83 research Associate with the Institute for History and Theory of Architecture, ETH, Zurich; concurrent work as independent architect; 1985-87 teaching assistant of Prof. Campi, ETH, Zurich; since 1987 own offices together with Markus Peter; Visiting Professor in Harvard and Zurich (together with M. Peter), 1992-94 Director of Design Comission, Feldkirch.

Markus Peter

1957, Zurich (Switzerland).

Studies at the Freie Universität, Berlin and study of architecture at the Technical Institute, Winterthur (Switzerland); 1985-86 architect in the offices of Prof. Schnebli; collaboration on Ruopigen Center, Lausanne; 1986-88 teaching assistant of Prof. Campi at the Federal Institute of Technology (ETH), Zurich.

MAJOR WORK Urban design study "Diagonal" of Barcelona (with Herzog & de Meuron), 1989; House Ruegg, 1994-95; Wooden bridge, Murau, Styria, 1995; Renovation of the main railway station, Zurich, 1996-97; cinema renovation, Zurich, 1997-98; technical specialist school, Biel (Switzerland), 1995-99.

Neururer & Neururer
Alois Neururer

1957, St Leonhardt, Tyrol.

Studied at the Technical University of Vienna; 1985-91 assistant to Prof. Ernst Hiesmayr; 1990-92 taught at the Technical University of Vienna; 1979-83 worked with W. Benedikt and 1985 with H. Puchhammer; since 1985 independent work in collaboration with Elena Theodorou-Neururer.

Elena Theodorou-Neururer

1959, Nicosia (Cyprus).

1977-84 studied at the Technical University of Vienna; 1977 received the Savidou Memorial Art Prize from the Cyprus; 1985-87 worked with Anton Schweighofer, Vienna; since 1985 collaborative work with Alois Neururer.

MAJOR WORK Renovation of residential buildings in Vienna (in collaboration with Atelier Zieglergasse), 1986-88; residential building renovation for Dr Konzett, Lower Austria, 1987-88; single family home for F. Geiszler, Vienna, 1987-89; residential building renovation for Dr Fink, Lower Austria, 1988-90; single family house Neururer, Tyrol, 1989-93; hotel complex project, Mandarfen, Tyrol, 1990; Vier Jahreszeiten (Four Seasons), Hotel Tyrol, 1990-91; Alpinhotel Mandarfen, 1990-92; residential housing complex, Wenns, Tyrol, 1992-94; single family house for Dr Neophytou, Lower Austria, 1994-96; residential housing complex, Imst-Arzill, Tyrol, 1994-96; Hotel Klinglhuber, Krems, Lower Austria, 1995-96.

Joseph Maria Olbrich

1867, Troppau — †1908 Düsseldorf (Germany).

Student of Prof. Karl von Hasenauer and Otto Wagner at the Academy of Fine Arts in Vienna; until 1898 worked in Wagner's studio; 1897 founding member of the Viennese Secession; 1899 was invited to work in the artists' colony in Darmstadt, Germany; 1908 moved to Düsseldorf.

MAJOR WORK Viennese Secession, exhibition building, 1897-98; mausoleum for the family Von Klarwillschen at the cemetery in Döbling, Vienna 1899; clubhouse pavilion for the civil servants' cycling club, 1899; Villa Friedmann, Hinterbrühl, Lower Austria, 1899; Villa Hermann Bahr, 1900; artists' colony at Mathildenhöhe, Darmstadt, 1900-02; residential and commercial building, Jägerndorf, 1904; warehouse Tietz, Düsseldorf, Germany, 1908.

Ortner & Ortner
Laurids Ortner
1941, Linz, Upper Austria.
1959-65 studied at the Technical University of Vienna; 1967 founded the artists' group Haus-Rucker-Co. in Vienna; 1970-87 collaborative work with Günther Zamp Kepp and Manfred Ortner in Düsseldorf; 1976-87 Professor at the University of Art and Industrial Design in Linz; since 1987 Professor at the State Art Academy in Düsseldorf; 1987 founded the architecture firm Ortner & Ortner with Manfred Ortner in Düsseldorf; since 1990 offices in Vienna and Linz.

Manfred Ortner
1943, Linz, Upper Austria.
1961-67 studied painting and art education at the Academy of Fine Arts in Vienna and history at the University of Vienna; 1966-71 taught art education; 1971-87 worked with the Haus-Rucker group in Düsseldorf.
MAJOR BUILDINGS AND PROJECTS Bene showrooms, Vienna, 1981; Bene office building and production halls, Waidhofen a. d. Ybbs, 1986-88; German Museum of History, Berlin, 1988; Nibelungen Bridge project, Linz, 1990; centre of the Brüser Berg city quarter in Bonn, 1991-93; renovation of the Landeszentralbank, Düsseldorf, 1992; department store M., Linz, 1992; European Design Depot - E.D.D., Klagenfurt, 1993-94; MAXX Hotel, Linz, 1994-95; building for the vocational school in Vienna, 1995; Museumsquartier (Museum Quarter), Vienna, 1997-2002; residential and commercial building, Berlin.

Gustav Peichl
1928, Vienna.
Student of Prof. Clemens Holzmeister; at the Academy of Fine Arts in Vienna; since 1956 freelance architect in Vienna; since 1955 political cartoonist working under

the pseudonym "Ironimus"; 1965 co-founder of the magazine BAU; 1969 Architecture Prize of the City of Vienna; 1971 Grand Austrian State Prize for Architecture; since 1973 Professor at the Academy of Fine Arts.
MAJOR WORK Administration building Newag, Maria Enzersdorf (in collaboration with W. Hubatsch, F. Kiener), 1959; "Atrium School", Döbling, Vienna, 1961-64; Austrian Pavilion at the World Fair in New York, 1964-65; Dominikanerinnen girls' boarding school, Hacking, Vienna, 1963-65; Rehabilitation Centre, Meidling, Vienna, 1965-68; ORF Centres (Austrian Public Television stations) Linz, Salzburg, Innsbruck, Dornbirn, 1970-72, Graz and Eisenstadt, 1978-81; ORF public broadcasting centre Kahlenberg, 1973; ground radio station Aflenz, 1976-79; Phosphate Elimination Plant, Tegel, Berlin, 1980-85; Villa Wienerberg, Vienna, 1985; German Art and Exhibition Hall Bonn, 1986-92; school at Wienerberg, Vienna, 1987-89; Städelmuseum extension, Frankfurt, 1987-90; EVN-Forum, Maria Enzersdorf, 1990-93; Akademiehof (academy courtyard) Karlsplatz, Vienna (in collaboration with Roland Rainer), 1993-96; elementary and junior high school, Vienna, 1994-96; sky scraper, Danube City, Vienna, 1994-97; Millennium Tower, Vienna (in collaboration with Boris Podrecca), 1997-99.

Jože (Josef) Plečnik
1872, Ljubljana (Slovenia) — †1957.
1888-92 carpentry apprenticeship; 1894 studied at the Academy of Fine Arts in Vienna, 1895-98 student of Prof. Otto Wagner; 1899-1900 worked in Wagner's office; until 1911 independent architect in Vienna; 1911-21 professor at the School of Applied Arts in Prague; from 1921 professor at the university in Ljubljana.
MAJOR WORK Zacherl Haus, Vienna, 1903-05; Church of the Holy Spirit, Vienna, 1910-13; renovation of the Prague Castle, 1920-34; church in Bogojina, 1925-27; Franziskanerkirche, church, Ljubljana, 1925-31; insurance agency building, Ljubljana (in collaboration with Ms Tomazic), 1930; Heart of Jesus Church, Prague, 1928-33; National and University Libraries, Ljubljana, 1939-41; St Anton Church, Belgrade, 1932-57.

Ernst Anton Plischke

1903, Klosterneuburg, Lower Austria – †1992, Vienna.
1921-23 student of Prof. Oskar Strnad at the Arts and
Crafts School and of Prof. Peter Behrens at the Academy
of Fine Arts; 1927-28 worked in Josef Frank's office;
from 1930 worked as a freelance architect; 1929-30
visited the United States; 1935 Grand Austrian State
Architecture Prize; 1939 emigrated to New Zealand;
1939-47 worked in the Ministry of Residential Housing;
from 1948 own office in Wellington; 1961 received
the Architecture Prize of the City of Vienna in absentia;
1963 returned to Vienna, Professor at the Academy
of Fine Arts, Vienna.

MAJOR WORK Interior design for an apartment for Lucie Rie,
Vienna, 1928; Bureau of Employment building, Liesing,
Vienna, 1930-32; house in the Vienna Woods, 1931;
two buildings in the in Viennese "Werkbundsiedlung",
1932; Bureau of Employment office, Gmünd, Lower
Austria, 1932-33; Bureau of Employment office,
Amstetten, Lower Austria, 1933-34; Gamerith House
on Lake Attersee, 1933-34.

MAJOR WORK (carried out in New Zealand after 1948) Central
administration building of the Dairy and Meat Board,
Wellington; Community Centre, Wellington; basilica
for the archbishop's seat in Wellington, modification
of its interior design.

Boris Podrecca

1941, Triest (Italy).
1960-67 studied at the Technical University and at
the Academy of Fine Arts in Vienna with Prof. Roland
Rainer; 1979-81 assistant at the Technical University
of Vienna and Munich; 1982-87 visiting professor in
Lausanne, Paris, Venice, London, Vienna and Harvard;
since 1988 professor at the Technical University of
Stuttgart; freelance architect in Vienna.

MAJOR WORK B. House, Vienna, 1980-82; design of the
Universitätsplatz, city square, Salzburg, 1986-91;
Kunsthalle (art exhibition centre project), Berlin, 1987;
Kika furniture store, Klagenfurt, 1988-89; urban
planning of the historical city centre of Como (Italy),
1989-90; exhibition hall in the Technical Museum,

Vienna, 1989; car showroom, Waidhofen a.d. Ybbs,
1990-92; Korotan Hotel and student residence, Vienna,
1990-95; bank office, Vienna, 1993-94; Dirmhirngasse
School, Vienna, 1992-94; "Ca Pesaro" Museum of
Modern Art, Venice (Italy), 1991-95; Kapellenweg
residential housing development, Vienna, 1986-89;
Biberach City Library (Germany), 1992-95; Basel
Insurance Company building, Vienna, 1993; residential
development at the Nordbahn (funicular railway) area,
Vienna, 1997-99; Millennium Tower, Vienna
(in collaboration with Gustav Peichl), 1997-99.

Alexander Popp

1891, St Leonhard a. Forst, Lower Austria – †1947, Linz.
Assistant to Prof. Peter Behrens at the Academy of
Fine Arts in Vienna; 1941-45 Professor at the Academy
of Fine Arts in Vienna; 1938-1941 chairman of the
commission at the Academy; 1931-1939 member of
the Viennese Secession.

MAJOR WORK DDSG Building, Belgrade, 1925; numerous
residential buildings in Vienna, 1928-30; worked with
Peter Behrens on the construction of the state tobacco
factory in Linz, 1929-1935; commercial and residential
building, Linz; Hermann-Göring-Werke, factory, Linz,
1938-43.

Carl Pruscha

1936, Innsbruck, Tyrol.
1955-60 studied at the Academy of Fine Arts in Vienna
and at Harvard University, USA; worked in Paul Lester's
and Wallace K. Harrison's offices in Vienna; 1964
member of the UN Council for Environmental Planning
and of UNESCO in Naples; several teaching positions in
the USA; since 1974 own office in Vienna; since 1978
professor at the Academy of Fine Arts in Vienna; since
1988 Dean at the Academy.

MAJOR WORK Renovation of the Schloss Neugebäude,
Simmering, Vienna; housing development
Biberhaufenweg, Vienna (in collaboration with Otto
Häuselmayer and Heinz Tesar), 1981-85; conversion of
the Piaristenkonvent (convent) into the Kunsthaus Horn
(exhibition area), 1988; residential housing development

Traviatagasse, Vienna (in collaboration with Raimand Abraham and others), 1988-91.

Roland Rainer

1910, Klagenfurt, Carinthia.
Studied at the Technical University of Vienna; 1935 doctoral thesis; 1953-54 professor for housing, urban development and landscaping at the Technical University in Hanover; 1954 Architecture Prize of the City of Vienna; 1956 Professor at the Academy of Fine Arts in Vienna (1960-62 Dean); 1958-63 City of Vienna's urban development councillor; 1962 Grand Austrian State Architecture Prize.

MAJOR WORK Numerous single family houses in Vienna; Freiluftschule Siebenhirten (open-air school), 1947; dormitories for apprentices, Vienna, 1952; Atelierhaus, Vienna, 1953; prefabricated housing development, Vienna (in collaboration with Carl Auböck), 1954; Stadthalle (sports stadium) Vienna, 1954-94; Böhler administrative building, Vienna, 1956-58; low building housing development, Vienna, 1961-63; Presbyterian church, Vienna, 1962-63; Stadthalle (stadium) Bremen (Germany), 1961-64; multipurpose hall, Ludwigshafen (Germany), 1961-63; Garden city: Gartenstadt Puchenau I, Linz, 1965-67; ORF Centre (Austrian Public Television) Küniglberg, Vienna, 1968-75; "Gartenstadt Puchnau II", Linz, 1977-98; Garden city: Gartenstadt Attnang-Puchheim, 1980; Documenta Urbana Kassel, 1982; numerous residental housing complexes in Vienna and Linz, 1985-96; Academy courtyard: Akademiehof Karlsplatz, Vienna, (in collaboration with Gustav Peichl), 1993-96.

Helmut Richter

1941, Styria.
Studied at the Technical University of Graz until 1968; 1969-71 studied computer science, systems and network theory at the University of California, Los Angeles (USA); 1971-1975 professor of architecture at the Ecole Nationale Superieure, Paris; 1976-1975 collaborative work with Heidulf Gerngross; 1977 founded the office Richter-Gerngross for "architecture – urban development-

organization - design - research" in Vienna; 1986 Professor at the Academy of Applied Arts in Vienna; 1986-87 Visiting Professor at the Gesamthochschule Kassel, since 1991 Professor at the Technical University of Vienna, department of structural engineering and design.

MAJOR WORK P. House, Wiener Neustadt (in collaboration with Heidulf Gerngross), 1978-89; Königseder House, Upper Austria (in collaboration with Heidulf Gerngross), 1980; Gräf & Sift residential building, Vienna, 1981-88; Restaurant Kiang I, Vienna, (with H.G.), 1984-85; Waidhausenstrasse School, Vienna, 1993-95; residential housing complex Brunnerstrasse, Vienna, 1986-91; Restaurant Kiang III, Vienna, 1996.

Max Rieder

1957, Salzburg.
1977-84 studied cultural technology and aquatic economics at the College for Agriculture in Vienna; 1980-86 student of Prof. Hans Hollein at the Academy of Applied Arts in Vienna; offices in Vienna and Salzburg.

MAJOR WORK Power plant, Salzburg; military complex Waldegg, Wiener Neustadt, Lower Austria; residential housing complex Wittgensteingründe, Vienna (in collaboration with Wolfgang Tschappeller and Hans Peter Wörndl), 1988-90; duplex Glanegg, Salzburg, 1990-92; Kindergarten Aigen, Salzburg; residential building Itzling, Salzburg 1995-97.

Riegler & Riewe
Florian Riegler

1954, Mönichwald, Styria.
Studied at the Technical University of Graz; since 1987 own office in Graz with Roger Riewe. Member of the Salzburg Council on Design; taught in Amsterdam, Aachen, Prague, Barcelona and Basel.

Roger Riewe

1959, Bielefeld (Germany).
Studied at the RWTH Aachen; since 1987 own office with Florian Riegler; 1987 Austrian Prize for Residential Housing.

MAJOR WORK Residential building, Mautern, Styria, 1988-92;

reconstruction of the CCW - Cultural Centre Wolkenstein, 1990; "Casa Nostra" residential housing complex, Graz, 1991-92; Cultural Centre Wolkenstein in Steinach, 1990; Graz Airport, 1992-94; residential building in Strassgang, Graz, 1992-94; Dr Hoff Sanatorium, Graz, 1997; State Institute for Social Education, Baden, Lower Austria, 1997-98; Technical University of Graz, computers & technology department, 1997-2000.

Peter Riepl
1952 Wels, Upper Austria.
Studied at the Technical University of Innsbruck.
Since 1985 own office. 1989 received the Culture Prize of the State of Upper Austria.

Thomas Moser
1954, Birgitz, Tyrol.
1987-94 collaborative work with Peter Riepl in Linz; since 1993 office together in Innsbruck; in 1995 Gabriele Riepl joined the office.
MAJOR WORK Computer Centre Hagenberg, Upper Austria, 1986-89; high school extension, Wels, Upper Austria 1991-94; multipurpose hall for the vocational school in Linz, 1992-95; Kindergarten, Linz, 1993-94; International Management Academy Bergschlössel in Linz; Bruckmühle Culture Center in Pregarten, Upper Austria; Ternberg City Hall, Upper Austria; numerous residential and office buildings; renovation and extension of the Offenes Kulturhaus (cultural centre) in Linz, 1995-98.

Hubert Riess
1946, Obernberg am Inn, Upper Austria.
1967-76 studied at the Technical University of Graz; since 1975 has been working independently; 1976-77 assistant to the visiting professor Jan Gezelius from Stockholm at the Technical University of Graz; 1978-79 scholarship to study in Stockholm, worked in Jan Gezelius's office; has been teaching at the Technical University of Graz since 1979; 1980 joined Ralph Erskine's firm; since 1985 own office in Graz; since 1994 Professor at the College for Architecture, Building and Construction at the University in Weimar.

MAJOR WORK Wooden house Dietmar Riess, 1973; residential housing complex Wienerbergründe, Graz (in collaboration with Ralph Erskine), 1982-87; Öttl House, Gerambose, 1985; residential housing development Knittelfeld, 1986-89; rental apartments, Graz, 1987-92; Cultural and Conference Centre, Judenburg, Styria, 1992-95.

Julius Schulte
1881, Steyrermühl, Upper Austria – †1928, Linz, Upper Austria.
Studied at the Technical University of Vienna with Prof. Max von Ferstel and Karl König; travelled through Belgium, Holland and Germany on study; 1909-21 councillor on urban development to the City of Linz; 1926 Professor at the Technical University of Graz.
MAJOR WORK Girls' high school, Linz, 1910-11; Raimand School, Linz, 1911-13; Weber School, Urfahr, Linz, 1911-13; Kindergarten Mauthausen, Upper Austria, 1914-15; State Fire Fighters' School, Linz, 1919; Traunfall Bridge, Steyrermühl, Upper Austria, 1924; housing development on Römerberg, Linz, 1923-28; housing development "Am Hang", Urfahr, Linz, 1926-27; Ebensee School, Upper Austria, 1927; Villa Seiler, Linz, 1927; Exerzitienheim Subiaco, dormitories, Kremsmünster, Upper Austria, 1928.

Franz Schuster
1892, Vienna – †1972, Vienna.
Student of Prof. Heinrich Tessenow and Oskar Strnad at the Arts and Crafts School of Vienna; moved to Dresden with Tessenow, worked on the landscaped residential housing development in Hellerau, Dresden; 1923-25 head architect of the Austrian Association for Residential Housing Development and Allotments; 1925 freelance architect in Vienna; 1926-27 taught at the Arts and Crafts School of Vienna; 1926 coeditor of the magazine "Der Aufbau"; 1928-36 worked as a freelance architect in Frankfurt; 1933-36 general secretary of the International Association for Residential Housing Development in Frankfurt; 1937 returned to Vienna; 1949 professor at the Academy of Applied Arts; 1951 Architecture Prize of the City of Vienna; from 1952-57 head of the research commission of the City of Vienna

in charge of residential housing; 1967 Grand Austrian State Prize for Architecture.

MAJOR WORK Otto-Haas-Hof, Vienna, 1924; Montessori Kindergarten, Vienna, 1926; Karl-Völkert-Hof, Vienna, 1926; collaboration in the interior design of various houses within the Weissenhof housing development, Stuttgart, Germany, 1927; adult education centre, Frankfurt/Main, 1928; Opelbad, Wiesbaden, Germany, 1932; Per-Albin-Hansson (West) housing development, Vienna (in collaboration with F. Pangratz, S. Simony, E. Wörle), 1947-51; Kindergarten "Schweizerspende", Vienna, 1948-49; housing development Siemensstrasse, Vienna, 1950-53; senior citizens home, Vienna, 1951-57; office building, Vienna, 1955-57; public outdoor swimming pool, Maarau/Rhein, Germany, 1963.

Karl Schwanzer

1918, Vienna — †1975, Vienna.
Studied at the Technical University of Vienna unitl 1941; 1947-51 assistant to Oswald Haerdtl; from 1949 independent architect in Vienna; 1958 Grand Prix for Architecture at the World Fair in Brussels; from 1959 Professor at the Technical University (1965-66 Dean); 1959 Architecture Prize of the City of Vienna, 1963 honorary member of the Royal Institute of Architects, and since 1967 of the American Institute of Architecture; Visiting Professor in Darmstadt, Budapest, and Riyad; received the Grand Austrian State Prize for Architecture posthumously.
MAJOR WORK Participated in building the residential housing complex Tivoligasse, Vienna 1957-58; First Viennese Car Lift, 1958; Austrian Pavilion and the European Pavilion at the World Fair in Brussels, 1958; Museum des 20. Jahrhunderts, art exhibition center and museum, Vienna, 1959-62; extension of the Kapuzine crypt, Vienna, 1959-60; Christkönigkirche, church, Vienna, 1960-63; Wirtschaftsförderungsinstitut (WIFI), Vienna, 1960-62; Philips administrative building, Vienna; 1962-63; extension of the Academy of Applied Arts in Vienna (in collaboration with Eugen Wörle), 1963-65; Austrian Pavilion at the World Fair in Montreal, 1966-67; hospital, Graz, 1968; BMW House, Munich, 1970-73; Austrian Embassy in Brasilia, Brazil, 1974.

Rudolf Schwarz

1897, Strasbourg — †1961, Cologne (Germany).
1915-19 student of Prof. Hans Poelzig at the Technical University of Berlin and at the State Academy of Arts; 1925-27 taught at the Arts and Crafts School in Offenbach, 1927-34 principal of the Arts and Crafts School in Aachen; 1934-40 freelance architect; 1946-52 general planner for the City of Cologne; 1953-61 professor for urban development at the Academy in Düsseldorf; 1958 Grand Art Prize from the State of Nordrhein-Westfalen, Germany.
MAJOR WORK Fronleichnamskirche, church, Aachen (in collaboration with Hans Schwippert), 1928-30; "Haus der Jugend", Aachen, 1929; church in Lichterfelde, Berlin, 1936; church in Fulda, 1938; girls' high school, Darmstadt, 1952; Maria-Königin-Kirche, church, Frechen (Germany), 1952-54; reconstruction of the Wallraf-Richartz-Museum, Cologne (with Josef Bernhard), 1955-56; Theresienkirche, church, Linz, 1958-62; Maria-Königin-Kirche, church, Saarbrücken, 1959; Pfarrkirche St Florian, parish church, Vienna, 1957-63.

Anton Schweighofer

1930, Ayancik (Turkey).
Student of Prof. Clemens Holzmeister at the Academy of Fine Arts in Vienna; worked in Austria, Sweden and Switzerland; since 1959 freelance architect; until 1964 collaborative work with Rupert Falkner; councillor for the International SOS Children's Village; since 1977 Professor at the Technical University of Vienna; 1977 Architecture Prize of the City of Vienna.
MAJOR WORK Mercedes Benz administrative building, Vienna (in collaboration with Peter Schweger), 1966; Kindergarten, Taegu, Korea, 1966; chapel at the SOS Childrens' Village, Hinterbrühl, 1967; elementary and junior high school, Allensteig, 1968; Schwesternhaus, convent, Zwettl, 1970; residential housing complex "Stadt des Kindes", Vienna, 1969-74; faculty building at the College of Agriculture, Vienna, 1974; hospital, Zwettl, Upper Austria, 1979; Konrad-Lorenz-Institute, Vienna, 1989-92; residence, St Andrä, Wördern, Lower Austria, 1992-93; student residence, Vienna, 1994-95; numerous residential housing complexes in Vienna.

Johannes Spalt

1920, Gmunden, Upper Austria.

Studied at the State Trade School in Salzburg; from 1945 offices in Gmunden and Vienna; 1949-52 studied at the Viennese Academy of Fine Arts with Prof. Clemens Holzmeister; 1950 founded Team 4 (see Team 4); 1967 taught at the Academy of Applied Arts; until 1970 collaborative work with Friedrich Kurrent; 1973 Architecture Prize of the City of Vienna; since 1973 Professor at the Academy of Applied Arts; buildings in collaboration with Team 4: see Team 4.

MAJOR WORK (in collaboration with Friedrich Kurrent) Wittmann, Etsdorf, Lower Austria, 1964-66; Terra-Baumaschinen AG, Vienna, 1964-67; interior design of the Neue Galerie gallery and of the secondary gallery of the Museum of Art History in Vienna, 1967-68; Z-Bank office, Floridsdorf, Vienna, 1970-74.

INDEPENDENT WORK Wittmann House, Etsdorf, Lower Austria, 1970-75; Salvatorkirche church, Vienna, 1976-79; numerous single family houses, including Draxler House, Vienna, 1987-88.

Splitterwerk

Markus Blaschitz 1965, **Johann Grabner** 1963, **Bernhard Kargl** 1965, **Gernot Ritter** 1968, **Josef Roschitz** 1964, **Markus Zechner** 1967.

Studied at the Technical University of Graz, and founded the architects' collective "Architekturwerkstatt Splitterwerk" 1988, working at the limits of architecture and art, won many competitions, for example with their "Prototyp Übelbach", a low-cost experimental piece of architecture with prefabricated elements which can be dismantled; residential building Hödlwald, Salzburg, 1994-96.

Otto Steidle

1943, Munich (Germany).

1962-65 studied at the State School of Architecture in Munich; 1965 studied at the Academy of Art in Munich; founded the office of Muhr & Steidle 1966; 1969 established the office Steidle & Partners in Munich; 1974 cofounder of the SEP (urban development planning); 1976 cofounder of the planning group for buildings for elementary and primary areas; 1979 Professor at the Polytechnic in Kassel; 1981 Professor at the Technical University of Berlin; Architecture Prize Berlin 1989; 1991 Visiting Professor at the Massachusetts Institute of Technology, Cambridge; 1991 Professor at the Academy of Fine Arts, Munich.

MAJOR WORK Terraced houses Munich, 1969-71; priests' centre, Erdweg, Dachau, 1971-72; apartments in terraced buildings, Munich, 1969-72; "Elementa" residential street, Nürnberg, 1972-74; plant apartments and dormitories for BMW, Dingolfing, Germany, 1973-74; St Michaelkirche church, Munich, 1978-79; housing development Pilotengasse, Vienna, 1989-92 (in collaboration with Adolf Krischanitz and Herzog & de Meuron); Documenta Urbana 1981; "Gartenstadt Heidemannstrasse", 1984; Gruner + Jahr publishing house, Hamburg, 1986-89 (with Uwe Kiessler); Wienerberg residential housing complexes, Vienna, 1989-93; University of Ulm, west wing, 1989-93.

Hans Steineder

1904, Linz, Upper Austria – †1976, Vienna.

1922-25 student of Prof. Peter Behrens at the Academy of Fine Arts in Vienna; worked as a freelance architect in Vienna and Linz after graduation.

MAJOR WORK Schulschwesternschule, school, Linz, 1927-29; "Kolpinghaus", Linz, 1930-32; residential building, Linz, 1930-32; girls' junior high school Vöcklabruck, Upper Austria, 1934-35; Marienkirche, church, Linz (with H. Koller-Buchwiesen), 1949-52; Neumargareten Church, Vienna (with H. Koller-Buchwiesen), 1949-52.

Karla Szyszkowitz-Kowalski

1944, Beuthen, Silesia.

1962-68 studied at the Technical University in Darmstadt; worked in Georges Candili's office in Paris; 1969-71 worked on the Olympia buildings for the architects Behnisch & Partner in Munich; 1971-72 taught at the Kassel polytechnic; 1973 started collaborative work with Michael Szyszkowitz, since 1978 shared office in Graz; 1988 professorship at the University of Stuttgart.

Michael Szyszkowitz

1944, Graz, Styria.

Studied at the Technical University of Graz;1970-71 worked on the planning of the Olympia buildings in Munich in Behnisch & Partner's office and in Domenig & Huth's office in Munich and Graz; since 1973 planning cooperative with Karla Kowalski; since 1978 shared office; 1987 cofounder of the House of Architecture in Graz.

MAJOR WORK Building overlooking Graz, Geidorf, Graz, 1973-75; funeral parlour Schwarzach, Salzburg, 1977-78; renovation of Grosslobming, Styria, 1978-81 and of Schloss Pichel, Styria, 1980-84; priests' centre, Graz-Ragnitz, 1982-87; residential housing complex, Eisbach-Reib, 1982-86; Institute for Biochemistry and Biotechnology at the Technical University of Graz, 1983-91; Graues Haus (grey house), Graz, 1985-86; residential housing complex Sandgasse, Graz, 1988-91; residential housing complex Knittelfeld, 1990-92; experimental residential housing complex, Stuttgart, 1989-93; elementary school Grosslobming, Styria 1994-96.

Heinz Tesar

1939, Innsbruck, Tyrol.

1961-65 student of Prof. Roland Rainer at the Academy of Fine Arts of Vienna; since 1973 freelance architect in Vienna; 1983 Architecture Prize of the City of Vienna; Visiting Professor at Cornell University, New York (1983), the ETH Zurich (1985-87), Mc Gill University, Montreal (1989), Harvard University, Cambridge (1990), the Technical University of Munich (1991-92), and the University of Minnesota, Minneapolis (1992).

MAJOR WORK Church, funeral parlour and cemetery Kleinarl, 1977-86; residential buildings Einsiedlergasse, Vienna, 1976-83, 1985-88; renovation of the parish church, Unternberg, 1976-79; fire department Perchtoldsdorf, Lower Austria, 1981-83; Grass House, Bregenz, 1981-83; housing development Biberhaufenweg, Vienna (in collaboration with Carl Pruscha and Otto Häuselmayer), 1981-85; administrative buildings Schömer, Klosterneuburg, Lower Austria, 1985-87; day care centre, Vienna, 1987-90; Stadttheater & Kino (theatre and cinema), Celtic Museum, Hallein, 1991-1996; semi-detached residential building Schömer, Klosterneuburg, Lower Austria, 1993-94; Protestant church, Klosterneuburg, Lower Austria, 1994-95; warehouse complex, St Gallen, Switzerland, 1995; Taschenberg Residence, Dresden, 1995.

Much Untertrifaller Sr

1933, Bozen, South Tyrol (Italy).

1952-55 worked in Hiesmayr & Gruber's office in Wolfurt; 1955-59 worked Strähli & Frehner's office in St Gallen, Switzerland; 1959-62 in Gerhard Hörburger's office in Bregenz; 1963 received his Master of Architecture and opened his own office in Bregenz; since 1978 collective with Gerhard Hörburger, since 1986 with Much Untertrifaller jr, and since 1993 with Helmut Dietrich.

Much Untertrifaller jr

1959, Bregenz.

Studied at the Technical University of Vienna; 1982-85 worked in Much Untertrifaller Sr's office; since 1986 office collective with Much Untertrifaller Sr; since 1993 with Helmut Dietrich as well.

MAJOR WORK Mittelweiherburg Elementary School, Hard, Vorarlberg, 1986 (with Much Untertrifaller Sr); Kindergarten Wolfurt-Dorf, Vorarlberg (with Helmut Dietrich), 1989-92; Bielerhöhe military base, Silvretta, Vorarlberg, 1991-92; Untertrifaller semi-detatched residential house, Bregenz, 1992-93; temporary Kindergarden, Lauterach, Vorarlberg (with Helmut Dietrich), 1992; Mäder School and Cultural Centre (with Helmut Dietrich); marina, Hard, Vorarlberg, 1993-94; festival theatre and convention centre Bregenz, extension (in collaboration with Helmut Dietrich), 1995-97.

Rudolf Wäger

1941, Götzis, Vorarlberg.

Carpenter, afterwards studied at the Academy of Fine Arts in Vienna for two semesters, student of Prof. Roland Rainer, own office in Feldkirch. Member of the "Gruppe Vorarlberger Baukünstler".

MAJOR WORK Since 1965 numerous single family houses in Vorarlberg; terraced house complex Ruhwiesen, Schlins, 1971-73; Rüdisser House, Hohenems, Vorarlberg, 1983-84; Kirche Maria Königin des Friedens, church, Dornbirn-Watzenegg, Vorarlberg (with Wolfgang Ritsch and Siegfried Wäger), 1984.

Otto Wagner

1841, Vienna — †1918.
1857-59 studied at the Technical University of Vienna; 1860 studied at the Academy of Architecture Berlin; 1861-63 student of Prof. August von Siccardsburg and Eduard van der Null at the Academy in Vienna; 1894-1913 Professor at the Academy of Fine Arts in Vienna, founding member of the Viennese Secession, member until 1905.
MAJOR WORK Länderbank, Vienna, 1882-84; first Wagner Villa, Vienna, 1886-88; rental apartment building, Universitätsstrasse 12, Vienna 1888; Palais Wagner, Vienna, 1889-91; "Ankerhaus", Vienna, 1894-95; Neumann warehouse, Vienna, 1895; Stadtbahn, local railway line in Vienna, and stations for the Stadtbahn, Vienna, 1894-1901; Nussdorf military complex, Vienna, 1894-1898; rental apartment buildings along the Linke Wienzeile 38-40; Vienna, 1898-99; office for the newspaper "Die Zeit", Vienna, 1902; church am Steinhof, Vienna, 1902-07; Staustufe Kaiserbad (luxury bath house), Vienna, 1904-08; Postsparkasse (postal savings bank), Vienna, 1903-06; rental apartment building, Neustiftgasse 40, Vienna, 1909-10; Lupus Pavilion, Wilhelminenspital, Vienna, 1910-13; rental apartment building, Vienna, 1911-12; second Wagner Villa, 1912-13.

Lois Welzenbacher

1889, Munich (Germany) — †1955, Absam.
1912-13 studied at the Technical University of Munich; from 1918 independent architect in Innsbruck and Munich; from 1922 taught at the State Trade School in Innsbruck; 1929-30 urban planning director of Plauen; 1939-45 responsible for industrial building planning in Halle/Saale; from 1947 Professor at the Academy of Fine Arts in Vienna.

MAJOR WORK Mimi Settari House, South Tyrol, 1922-23; Hotel and Café Reisch, Kitzbühel, Tyrol, 1922-23; electricity plant administrative building, Innsbruck, 1926-27; Schulz House, Recklinghausen, Germany, 1928-29; Rosenbauer House, Linz, 1929-30; Treichl House, Innsbruck, 1929-31; Turmhotel Seeber, Hall, 1930-31; Adambräu brewery, Innsbruck, 1931; Heyrovsky House, Thumersbach/Zell am See, 1932; day care centre Ehlert, Hindelang/Allgäu, 1931-33; urban development projects for Antwerp and Vienna.

Ludwig Wittgenstein

1889, Vienna — †1951, Cambridge (England).
1906-1911 studied mechanical engineering in Berlin and in Manchester; from 1912 studied mathematical logic as student of Prof. Bertrand Russell in Cambridge; 1914-1918 volunteered for WWI; 1919-26 taught in a state school; 1922 publication of the German edition of his "Tractatus logico-philosophicus"; 1939-47 Professor in Cambridge.
MAJOR WORK Stonborough-Wittgenstein House, Vienna (in collaboration with Paul Engelmann), 1926-28.

Oskar Wlach

1881, Vienna — †1963, New York (USA).
Studied at the Technical University of Vienna, 1906 dissertation; collaborative work with Oskar Strnad and Josef Frank; 1925 founded the furnishing company "Haus & Garten" in collaboration with Josef Frank; 1938 emigrated to New York.
MAJOR WORK Hock House, Vienna (in collaboration with Oskar Strnad), 1910-12; residential building Stuckgasse, Vienna (with Oskar Strnad), 1910-12; Wassermann House, Vienna (with Oskar Strnad and Josef Frank), 1914; residential housing complex Gellertgasse, Vienna, 1926; Beer House, Vienna (with Josef Frank), 1929-30; two houses in the Viennese "Werkbundsiedlung", 1932; residential housing complex Simmeringer Hauptstrasse, Vienna, 1932; Bunzl House, Vienna (with Josef Frank), 1936.

Manfred Wolff-Plottegg

1946, Schöder-Murau, Styria.

Studied at the Technical University of Graz; scholarship to the Ecole des Beaux Arts in Paris; postgraduate studies at the University of Economics in Vienna; adviser for various construction companies; assistant at the Technical University of Graz; member of the commission of specialists on the historical area of the city of Graz; taught computer conception at the University of Art and Industrial Design, Linz.

MAJOR WORK Apartment renovation, Vienna, 1979; general rebuilding of Schloss Trautenfels, Styria, 1988-92; attic renovations, Graz, 1987-91; housing complex Seiersberg, Graz, 1987-96; housing complex, Leoben, 1992; bath house, transparent changing rooms, Graz, 1993; since 1982 has been working on the topic "bathroom" and has done interior design for numerous bathrooms.

Eugen Wörle

1909, Vienna – †1996.

Student of Prof. Clemens Holzmeister at the Academy of Fine Arts in Vienna; worked for Clemens Holzmeister and Max Fellerer; 1936-42 and 1945-57 work cooperative with Max Fellerer; 1956 Architecture Prize of the City of Vienna; since 1957 own office in Vienna. Major buildings in collaboration with Max Fellerer: see Max Fellerer.

INDEPENDENT WORK Extension of Academy of Applied Arts, Vienna (in collaboration with Karl Schwanzer), 1960-65; Lugeck House, Vienna (with Bruno Doskar), 1961-62; residential housing complexes Goldene Stiege, Mödling, 1967-70 and Auhofstrasse, Vienna 1969-72; elementary, junior high school and special education school of the City of Vienna (with Ferry Kitt), 1970-71.

Hans Peter Wörndl

1958, Salzburg.

Studied architecture at the Technical University of Munich, 1982 graduated from Prof. Friedrich Kurrent's masterclass; 1984-85 postgraduate studies at the Cornell University, Ithaca, New York (USA). Worked with Heinz Tesar and Coop Himmelb(l)au; 1984 founded RTW,

a non-binding partnership with Max Rieder and Wolfgang Tschapeller.

MAJOR WORK Residential building Wittgensteingründe, Vienna (in collaboration with Max Rieder and Wolfgang Tschapeller), 1985-90; GucklHupf, Kulturbox (culture box) am Mondsee, Salzburg, 1992; single family houses in Salzburg, 1991 and 1995; several residential buildings, Salzburg, 1996-99.

Fritz Wotruba

1907, Vienna – †1975, Vienna.

1922-23 Life class at the Arts and Crafts School in Vienna; 1936-28 student of Anton Hanak, major in sculpture; 1932 Austrian representative at the Biennale in Venice; 1934 emigrated to Switzerland; 1945 returned to Austria; Professor at the Viennese Academy of Fine Arts; 1950 participated at the Biennale in Venice. Grand Austrian State Prize for Architecture.

MAJOR WORK Figural relief for the Austrian Pavilion at the World Fair in Brussels, 1958; Church "Zur heiligsten Dreifaltigkeit" in Vienna (in collaboration with Fritz Gerhard Mayr), 1965-76.

Peter Zumthor

1943, Basel (Switzerland).

Carpentry apprenticeship specializing in furniture; from 1963 studied at the School of Design in Basel and at the Pratt Institute in New York; 1978 taught at the University of Zurich; since 1979 own architecture office; 1988 Visiting Professor at the Southern California Institute of Architecture, Santa Monica, Los Angeles (USA); 1989 Visiting Professor at the Technical University of Munich.

MAJOR WORK Räth House, Haldenstein, 1983; Zumthor Studio, Haldenstein (Switzerland), 1985-86; Sogn Benedetg Chapel, Sumvitg, 1985-88; house for senior citizens, Masans (Switzerland), 1989-93; Art Museum Chur (Switzerland) (in collaboration with P. Calonder and H.J. Rauch), 1990; thermal bath and spa, Vals (Switzerland), 1993-1996; Kunsthaus (art exhibition centre), Bregenz, 1989-1997; Kolumba - arch-diocesan museum, Cologne (Germany), 1997-.

A.20.J.	*Architektur des 20. Jahrhunderts*
	(20th-century architecture), Berlin
A.A.	Archives of the Architect(s)
A.AZW.	Archives of the Architektur Zentrum Wien
A.B.	Archive Barth
A.Be.	Adolf Bereuter
A.C.	Archives Czech
A.D.	Archives Domenig
A.D.S.	Archives Dietmar Steiner
A.F.A.	Archives Friedrich Achleitner
A.F.W.	Association for the preservation and caretaking
	of Fritz Wotruba's legacy
A.G.	Archives Garstenauer
A.Gs.	Archives Gsteu
A.H.	Archives Hiesmayr
A.Ho.	Archives Hollein
A.K.	Angelo Kaunat
A.Ka.	Archives Kada
A.Ko.	Archive Kovatsch
A.L.,K.	Archives Loudon, Koch
A.M.L.	Architecture Museum Laibach
A.N.L.,V.	Austrian National Library, Vienna
A.P.	Archives Peichl
A.P.S.B.,V.	Austrian Postal Savings Bank, Vienna
A.R.	Archives Rainer
A.Ri.	Archive Richter
A.T.,L.	Austria Tabakwerke, Linz
A.V.S.	Archives of the Vienna Secession
B.H.	Bernhard Hafner
C.A.A.	Collection Alessandro Alverá
C.H.	Clemens Holzmeister
C.L.	Christof Lackner
C.S.	Christian Schepe
D.C.	Daniele Consolascio
D.L.	Dieter Leistner
D.n.T.,L.	*Die neue Tabakfabrik in Linz*
E.H.	Eduard Hueber
E.W.	Erich Widder
F.A.	Friedrich Achleitner
F.H.	Franz Hubmann
F.W.	Franz Wimmer
G.C.A.G.,V.	Graphic Collection of the Albertina Gallery, Vienna
G.H.AG,S.	Grossglockner Hochalpenstrasse AG
	(Association of Alpine Roads), Salzburg

G.U.	Gerhard Ullmann
G.v.B.	Gert von Bassewitz
G.Z.	Gerald Zugmann
H.G.T.	Hans Gregor Tropper
H.H.	Hertha Hurnaus
H.M.,V.	Historical Museum, Vienna
H.R.	Hans Rathmanner
H.S.	Herbert Schwingenschloegl
I.M.	Ignacio Martínez
J.P.	Josef Pausch
K.K.	Klaus Kostadedoi
K.M.	Karin Mack
L.C.	Lucca Chmel
L.H.,AZW.	Legacy Haerdtl, Architektur Zentrum Wien
L.S.	Legacy Steineder
L.W.	Legacy Woerle
M.20 C.,V.	Museum of the 20th Century, Vienna
M.A.V.	Municipal Authorities of the city of Vienna
M.B.	*Moderne Bauformen*
M.E.	Mischa Erben
M.G.	Martin Gerlach
M.G.,G.C.A.G.,V.	Martin Gerlach, Graphic Collection
	of the Albertina Gallery, Vienna
M.G.,H.M.	Martin Gerlach, Historisches Museum
M.M.	Michael Mauracher
M.N	Moritz Nähr
M.P.-D.	Martha Popp-Deltsios
M.S.	Margherita Spiluttini
Ö.B.W.	*Österreichische Bau- und Werkkunst*
P.O.	Paul Ott
P.W.	Peter Winklehner
R.S.	Rupert Steiner
R.W.	Rudolf Wäger
S.F.&H.G.	S.F. & H. Group
S.S.	Sophie Seitz
T.C.M.F.	Tyrol Community Museum "Ferdinandeum"
T.M.	Toni Muhr
T.U.I.	Technical University of Innsbruck
U.A.A.,V.	University of Applied Arts, Vienna
U.F.A.,V.	University of Fine Arts, Vienna
W.K.	Werner Kaligofsky
W.Ko.	Wilmar Koenig

Architecture in Austria.
A Survey of the 20th Century.

Publishers
Birkhäuser - Publishers for Architecture, Basel
ACTAR, Barcelona

Concept
Otto Kapfinger, Dietmar Steiner, Adolph Stiller

Editors
Sasha Pirker, Architektur Zentrum Wien
Jaime Salazar, ACTAR

Texts
Otto Kapfinger, Dietmar Steiner, Sasha Pirker

Translations
BrainStorm Vienna, Marion Kuzmany, Julian Cooper

Graphic Design
Ramon Prat, David Lorente

Production
Font i Prat Ass.

Printing
Ingoprint SA. Barcelona

Distribution
Birkhäuser
Publishers for Architecture
P.O. Box 133
CH - 4010 Basel

Tel: +41/61/2050-707
Fax: +41/61/2050-792
e-mail: promotion@birkhauser.ch
http://www.birkhauser.ch

Back cover photograph:
Alpine peaks (Austria)
© Bernard Roussel (The Image Bank)

A CIP catalogue record for this book is available from the
Library of Congress, Washington D.C., USA

Deutsche Bibliothek Cataloging-in-Publication Data

Architecture in Austria : a survey of the 20th century /
Architektur Zentrum Wien. Mit einer Einl. von Otto Kapfinger
und einem Vorw. von Dietmar Steiner. Aus dem Dt. ins Engl.:
Kuzmany, Marion ; Cooper, Julian. - Basel ; Boston ; Berlin :
Birkhäuser, 1999
ISBN 3-7643-6031-3

© 1999 ACTAR Publishers, Roca i Batlle 2-4, E-08023
Barcelona, Spain, and Birkhäuser - Publishers for Architecture,
P.O. Box 133, CH-4010 Basel, Switzerland.
Printed on acid-free paper produced from chlorine-free pulp.
TCF ∞

Printed in Spain
ISBN 3-7643-6031-3
ISBN 0-8176-6031-3

9 8 7 6 5 4 3 2 1